The Mainstay

Concerning Jurisprudence

[al-ʿUmda fi 'l-Fiqh]

Wafajjarnā khilālalahumā nahara, "And we caused a river to gush forth therein." (Q 18:33)

Cover calligraphy: Rohana Filippi

Using watercolor and wax to combine the beauty of Arabic script with the Qur'ānic message on paper, Italian artist Rohana Filippi has developed her own artistic style through personal research and inner inspiration. Her art is entirely devoted to "expressing Allāh's presence everywhere."

Ms. Filippi, who currently resides in Canada, has lived and worked in England, Mexico, Colombia and the United States.

Cover Design: .... Dryden Design, Houston, Texas
Cover Preparation: .... Indigo Design, Inc, Ft. Lauderdale, Florida
Typesetting: .... Indigo Design, Inc, Ft. Lauderdale, Florida

Body text set entirely in Ghazali & Jilani font by Al-Baz Publishing, Inc.

Library of Congress
Catalog Card Number: 2008941123

ISBN: 9781882216246

Published by Al-Baz Publishing, Inc.
1516 NE 38th Street
Oakland Park, FL 33334
Phone: (425) 891-5444
Fax: (954) 981-7304 E-mail: albaz@bellsouth.net

Printed and bound in the U.S.A. by Sheridan Books, Inc. Ann Arbor, MI.

The Mainstay

Concerning Jurisprudence

[al-ʿUmda fi 'l-Fiqh]

Concerning the Jurisprudence of the Imām of the Sunna,
Aḥmad ibn Ḥanbal ash-Shaibānī
(may Allāh be well pleased with him)

by
Imām Muwaffaq ad-Dīn ʿAbdu'llāh ibn Aḥmad
ibn Qudāma al-Maqdisī
(A.H. 541–620)

Translated from the Arabic by
Muhtar Holland

AL-BAZ PUBLISHING, INC.
FORT LAUDERDALE, FLORIDA

Contents

Biography of Shaikh al-Islām al-Muwaffaq, the Author of al-ʿUmda [the Mainstay]

(A.H. 541–620)

He is the devoutly diligent Imām, the Shaikh of Islām and one of the luminaries, Muwaffaq ad-Dīn Abū Muḥammad ʿAbdu'llāh ibn Aḥmad ibn Muḥammad ibn Qudāma ibn Miqdām ibn Naṣr ibn ʿAbdi'llāh ibn Ḥudhaifa ibn Muḥammad ibn Yaʿqūb ibn al-Qāsim ibn Ibrāhīm ibn Ismāʿīl ibn Yaḥyā ibn Muḥammad ibn Sālim ibn aṣ-Ṣaḥābī al-Jalīl [the Glorious Companion] ʿAbdi'llāh ibn Amīr al-Muʾminīn [the Commander of the Believers] ʿUmār ibn al-Khaṭṭāb al-ʿAdawī al-Qurashī.

He was born in the town of Jammāʿīl, one of the provincial districts of Nablus in Palestine, in the month of Shaʿbān, A.H. 541. When he was in the eighth year of his life, the Crusaders seized control of the blessed country, which had previously been governed by aẓ-Ẓāfir al-ʿUbaidī, so al-Muwaffaq's father emigrated with his family to Damascus, around the year A.H. 551, and they camped in the Mosque of Abū Ṣāliḥ outside the Eastern Gate. Then, after two years, they moved from the Ṣāliḥiyya quarter of Damascus to the foothill of Mount Qāsiyūn, in the Ṣalāḥiyya quarter of Damascus

Throughout this period, al-Muwaffaq was preoccupied with memorizing the Qurʾān, the rudiments of the religious sciences, and the texts of the Ḥanbalī school of jurisprudence, including the *Mukhtaṣar* [Compendium] of al-Kharaqī. Among his fellow students at that time, those of his own age included his maternal cousin, al-Ḥāfiẓ Taqī ad-Dīn ʿAbd al-Ghanī ibn ʿAbd al-Wāḥid al-Jammāʿīlī (A.H. 541–600) and his brother, ʿImād ad-Dīn Ibrāhīm ibn ʿAbd al-Wāḥid (A.H. 543–614), while al-Muwaffaq's own brother, Shaikh Abū ʿUmar (A.H. 528–607) was older than them.

The head of the family, Shaikh Abu 'l-ʿAbbās Aḥmad ibn Muḥammad ibn Qudāma (the father of al-Muwaffaq and Abū ʿUmar), was one of the masters of knowledge and righteousness. Before his migration to Damascus, he was the preacher of Jammāʿīl, its scholar and its pious ascetic. He was the first teacher of Shaikh al-Muwaffaq, of his brother before him, of their two maternal cousins, al-Ḥāfiẓ ʿAbd al-Ghanī and his brother al-ʿImād Ibrāhīm, and of all the other lion cubs of this fine house.

In the next stage, al-Muwaffaq studied under the Shaikhs of Damascus, including Abu 'l-Makārim ʿAbd al-Wāḥid ibn Abī Ṭāhir Muḥammad ibn al-Muslim ibn al-Ḥasan ibn Hilāl al-Azdī ad-Dimashqī, who died in the month of Jumādā 'l-Ākhira, A.H. 565, and Abu 'l-Maʿālī ʿAbdu'llāh ibn ʿAbd ar-Raḥmān ibn Aḥmad ibn ʿAlī ibn Ṣābir ad-Dimashqī (A.H. 499–576).

He did not cease to make progress in learning and the training of the lower self, until he reached the age of twenty. Then, between the years A.H. 560 and 561, he embarked on a educational expedition to Baghdād, accompanied by his maternal cousin Shaikh ʿAbd al-Ghanī (they were both of the same age). At the outset of his career, al-Muwaffaq spent a brief period in the presence of Shaikh ʿAbd al-Qādir al-Jīlānī, at his college in Baghdād. Under the Shaikh, who was then in the ninetieth year his life, he studied the *Mukhtaṣar* [Compendium] of al-Kharaqī at the level of understanding and meticulous scrutiny, because he had memorized the *Mukhtaṣar* while he was in Damascus. Shaikh ʿAbd al-Qādir completed his earthly life shortly after that, on the 8th of Rabiʿ al-Ākhir in the year A.H. 561, so al-Muwaffaq turned to the Shaikh of the Ḥanbalīs and the leading jurist of ʿIrāq, Nāṣiḥ al-Islām Abu 'l-Fatḥ Naṣr ibn Fityān ibn Maṭar an-Nahrawānī, well-known as Ibn al-Munā (A.H. 477–564). Under him he studied the jurisprudence of the school of Imām Aḥmad [ibn Ḥanbal], the subjects of disagreement, and the science of the basic principles of Islāmic law. He stayed in Baghdād for four years, during which he attended lectures given by the following authorities:

- The Pillar of ʿIrāq, Hibatu'llāh al-Ḥasan ibn Hilāl ad-Daqqāq (A.H. 472–562).
- Shaikh al-Masnad Abu 'l-Fatḥ Muḥammad ibn ʿAbd al-Bāqī ibn Aḥmad ibn Sulaimān, well-known as Ibn al-Baṭā al-Baghdādī (A.H. 477–564).
- The jurist, preacher, Qurʾān-reciter and man of letters, Abu 'l-Ḥasan Muhadhdhab ad-Dīn Saʿdu'llāh ibn Naṣr ibn Saʿīd, well known as Ibn ad-Dajjājī (A.H. 482–564).
- The Qurʾān-memorizer, jurist and reliable historian, Abu 'l-Faḍl Aḥmad ibn Ṣāliḥ ibn Shāfiʿ al-Jīlī / al-Baghdādī al-Ḥanbalī (A.H. 520–565).
- The expert in Prophetic tradition, Shaikh Abū Ṭālib al-Mubārak ibn Khaḍīr ibn ʿAlī aṣ-Ṣairafī al-Baghdādī (A.H. 482–562).
- The reliable transmitter of Prophetic tradition, Shaikh Abū Bakr ʿAbdu'llāh ibn Muḥammad ibn Abi 'l-Ḥusain Aḥmad ibn Muḥammad ibn an-Naqūr al-Bazzār (A.H. 483–565).
- The pride of the women, the authoritative female writer, Shahda bint Naṣr Aḥmad ibn al-Faraj ad-Dīnūrī/al-Baghdādī (A.H. 480–574).
- Many others from among the luminaries and scholars of Baghdād.

He seems to have returned from Baghdād to Damascus by way of Mosul, for he received instruction there from its orator, Abu 'l-Faḍl.

According to his sister's son, aḍ-Ḍiyāʾ al-Maqdisī (A.H. 569–643), the author of *al-Mukhtāra* [the Anthology], he heard his mother, al-Muwaffaq's sister, say: "The duration of al-Muwaffaq's stay in Baghdād was approximately four years. Then he returned to Damascus and renewed his connection with it and with his relatives there."

As reported by al-Ḥāfiẓ Ibn Rajab in the appendix to *Ṭabaqāt al-Ḥanābila* [The Ranks of the Ḥanbalīs], on the authority of the grandson of Ibn al-Jawzī (A.H. 581–654), al-Muwaffaq returned to Baghdād in the year A.H. 567.

Ibn Rajab said: "According to an-Nāṣiḥ ibn al-Ḥanbalī, otherwise known as ʿAbd ar-Raḥmān ibn Najm as-Saʿdī (A.H. 554–634), al-Muwaffaq performed the Pilgrimage in the year A.H. 574. He returned to Baghdād with the delegation of ʿIrāq, and stayed there for a year, so he attended the lectures of Ibn al-Munā." As quoted by Ibn Rajab, an-Nāṣiḥ ibn al-Ḥanbalī said: "I had entered Baghdād in the year A.H. 572, and we studied together under Shaikh Abu 'l-Fatḥ ibn al-Munā."

In the Meccan Sanctuary during the Pilgrimage of the year A.H. 574, al-Muwaffaq met the Imām of the Ḥanbalīs, al-Ḥāfiẓ al-Muḥaddith Abū Muḥammad al-Mubārak ibn ʿAlī ibn al-Ḥusain ibn ʿAbdi'llāh ibn Muḥammad aṭ-Ṭabbākh al-Baghdādī, a resident of Mecca who died there during the Festival of Breaking Fast *[ʿĪd al-Fiṭr]* in the year A.H. 575, so he received instruction from him.

Imām al-Muwaffaq settled in Damascus after these travels of his, and there he preoccupied himself with the composition of his great commentary (*al-Mughnī*) on al-Kharaqī's *Mukhtaṣar*. That is the copious commentary from which there developed an encyclopedia of Islāmic jurisprudence, containing articles and detailed notes by which the generations will benefit until the Day of Resurrection.

The biography of al-Muwaffaq is too vast to be contained within the preface of a book. It was treated as a separate subject by his maternal cousin, al-Ḥāfiẓ Ḍiyāʾ ad-Dīn as-Saʿdī, in a work compiled in two parts. A book on the biography of this great Imām was also compiled by al-Ḥāfiẓ adh-Dhahabī.

Throughout the time of Imām al-Muwaffaq's preoccupation with his literary works—of which we shall list the principal items—the seekers of knowledge would receive lectures from him from the early morning till the high point of the day. Then they would study under him after the midday prayer until the afternoon prayer, and after the afternoon prayer until the sunset prayer, learning either from the Prophetic tradition or from his literary compositions.

Many people have acquired their knowledge of jurisprudence from these works, including his brother's son, Chief Justice Shams ad-Dīn ʿAbd ar-Raḥmān ibn Abī ʿUmar (A.H. 597–682) and his generation, as well as the latter's much earlier predecessor, the commentator on *al-ʿUmda*, Bahāʾ ad-Dīn ʿAbd ar-Raḥmān ibn Ibrāhīm as-Saʿdī (A.H. 556–682) and his generation, not to mention the names of countless beneficiaries between those generations, among the scholars, the jurists, the distinguished experts in Prophetic tradition, and the bearers of the trusts of the Muḥammadan Sunna. His meeting room was always filled to capacity with jurists, experts in Prophetic tradition, and people of virtuous character.

In addition to this, and despite his constant commitment to literary composition, he used to recite one-seventh of the Qur'ān every day and night. As part of his regular practice, after leading the people in the obligatory ritual prayers in the mosque, he would usually refrain from performing the customary ritual prayer until he was at home, in accordance with the Sunna.

The more he advanced in years, the more he was endowed by Allāh with knowledge, grace, righteousness, modest humility, noble traits of character, and abstinence from this world and its phenomena, until he came to be counted among the great leaders of the Muslims, in worshipful service, true devotion, jurisprudence, the Prophetic tradition, and the basic principles of the religion, as well as the sciences of the Arabic language, the distribution of inherited estates, mathematics, and the times appointed [for the performance of religious duties].

Shaikh al-Islām ibn Taimiyya said about him: "After al-Awzā'ī, no one more expert in jurisprudence than Shaikh Muwaffaq has ever entered Damascus!" That is a testimony from the bearer of the trusts of Islām, the custodian of its realities, so it carries more weight than all the acclamations of this world.

According to the historian Shams ad-Dīn Yūsuf, the grandson of Ibn al-Jawzī (A.H. 581–654), in his book entitled *Mir'āt az-Zamān* [The Mirror of the Time]: "Al-Muwaffaq was a leader in many fields. No one in his time—after his brother Abū 'Umar and [his cousin] al-'Imād—was more abstinent or more piously cautious than he. He was very modest, averse to this world and its people, simple, gentle and humble, fond of the needy, endowed with virtuous characteristics, generous and munificent. Whenever someone saw him, it was as if he had seen one of the Companions, and light seemed to emanate from his face."

Shams ad-Dīn Yūsuf also said: "From Shaikh Abū 'Umar, his brother al-Muwaffaq and his cousin al-'Imād, I witnessed what we attribute to the Companions and the extraordinary saints, so their condition made me forget my family and my fellow countrymen, but then I returned to them with the intention of staying. Perhaps I shall be with them in the abode of permanent residence [in the Hereafter]!"

Muḥibb ad-Dīn Muḥammad ibn Maḥmūd ibn an-Najjār (A.H. 578–643) described him in the appendix to the *History of Baghdād*, for he said:

"Shaikh Muwaffaq ad-Dīn was the prayer leader of the Ḥanbalīs in the congregational mosque. He was trustworthy, magnanimous, extremely gracious, perfectly intelligent, intensely circumspect, constantly calm and composed, well-mannered, decent, piously cautious, devoted to worship in accordance with the statute of the righteous predecessors. Light glowed on his face, and he was endowed with dignity and reverence. Any man would benefit by the very sight of him, before hearing his speech."

The historian of the reign of Saladin, Shihāb ad-Dīn Abu 'l-Qāsim ʿAbd ar-Raḥmān ibn Ismāʿīl ibn Shāma al-Maqdisī ad-Dimashqī (A.H. 596–665), was one of those who attended his lectures and learned from him. He said: "The Shaikh of the Ḥanbalīs, Muwaffaq ad-Dīn, was one of the leaders of the Muslims and one of the luminaries of the religion, in both knowledge and practice.... King al-ʿAzīz ibn al-ʿĀdil once came to visit him. He arrived to find him performing the ritual prayer, so he sat close beside him until he finished his prayer, without speeding it up, then met with him.... After finishing ritual prayer of the late afternoon, he would walk to his house by the causeway, accompanied by as many of the local paupers as Allāh (Exalted is He) decreed, so he would provide them with something for them to eat with him."

According to the author of *al-Mukhtaṣar*, the great Qurʾān-memorizer Ḍiyāʾ as-Dīn Abū ʿAbdi'llāh Muḥammad ibn ʿAbd al-Wāḥid as-Saʿdī al-Maqdisī (A.H. 569–643), who was the son of Imām al-Muwaffaq's sister: "Al-Muwaffaq (may Allāh bestow His mercy upon him) was an Imām in the field of the Qurʾān and its exegesis; an Imām in the science of the Prophetic tradition and its problems; an Imām in jurisprudence, or rather, its unique exponent in his time; an Imām in the science of controversy; an Imām in the distribution of inherited estates; an Imām in the basic principles of jurisprudence; an Imām in grammar; an Imām in mathematics; an Imām in astronomy. When he arrived in Baghdād, Shaikh Abu 'l-Fatḥ ibn al-Munā said to him: 'You should take up residence here, for Baghdād is sorely in need of you, but you will depart from Baghdād without leaving anyone like you to replace you in it!'"

According to the same source: "Our Shaikh al-ʿImād (A.H. 543–614) holds Shaikh al-Muwaffaq in very high esteem. He invokes blessing upon him, him and sits in his presence like a student sitting in the presence of his teacher. I heard the Imām and Muftī, our Shaikh Abū Bakr Muḥammad ibn Maʿālī ibn Ghunaima, say: 'I do not know anyone in our time who has attained to the degree of independent judgment *[ijtihād]*, with the exception of al-Muwaffaq.' I heard Abū ʿAmr ibn aṣ-Ṣalāḥ say: 'I have never seen the like of Shaikh al-Muwaffaq!' Shaikh ʿAbdu'llāh al-Yūnainī (A.H. 535–617) said: 'I do not believe that any person, of all those I have seen, has acquired such perfection in the sciences, and the praiseworthy attributes by which perfection is acquired, apart from him. He (may Allāh bestow His mercy upon him) was perfect in his outer form and his inner content, in goodness and beneficence, tolerance and dignity, the various sciences, fine traits of character, and matters that I have never seen perfected in anyone but him.'"

On Friday, the Day of Congregation, Shaikh al-Muwaffaq used to convene a circle in the congregational Mosque of Banī Umayya in Damascus, in order to conduct a debate, after the ritual prayer, about all the questions and problems of religious science. He abstained from that, however, in the latter part of his life. They said: "He would not argue with anyone without smiling, to the point where someone said: 'This Shaikh kills his adversary with his smile!'" In his debates, he would appoint the texts of the Sacred Law to serve as the referee between him and his opponents. He would not engage with them in the controversy of the theologians and the hypocrites. According to al-Ḥāfiẓ Ibn Rajab, in the biography of al-Muwaffaq provided in his appendix to *Ṭabaqāt al-Ḥanābila* [The Ranks of the Hanbalīs]: "He did not consider it appropriate to plunge into debate with the theologians concerning the subtleties of theology, not even to refute them. He was very attentive to discussion on the subject of the roots [of Islāmic law] and other relevant topics. He would not accept the expression of unsubstantiated statements, and he would insist on confirmation and citation of the Divine attributes revealed in the Book and the Sunna, without commentary or qualification, without comparison or distortion, and without interpretation or negation."

When Ṣalāḥ ad-Dīn [Saladin] Yūsuf ibn Ayyūb mobilized the armies of Islām in the year A.H. 583, for the purpose of routing the Crusaders and purifying the Holy Land by ridding it of them, Imām al-Muwaffaq, his brother Shaikh Abū ʿUmar, the young men of their family, and the noble disciples of this house, were among the warriors beneath these victorious banners. Shaikh Abū ʿUmar was at the age of fifty-five, while Shaikh al-Muwaffaq was in his forty-second year. They and élite of their disciples had a tent, in which they met together with the warriors in the cause of Allāh. Both of them were the focus of respect and attention from King al-ʿĀdil, the son of Sulṭān Ṣalāḥ ad-Dīn. Al-Muwaffaq later enjoyed that same respect and attention, and even more, from King al-ʿAzīz, the son of King al-ʿĀdil.

Shaikh Abū ʿUmar used to lead the prayer and deliver the Friday sermon in the Muẓaffarī Congregational Mosque. When he died in the year A.H. 607, Imām al-Muwaffaq performed that duty. Whenever he was absent from the Muẓaffarī Congregational Mosque, the role of prayer leader and orator was assumed by Shaikh Sharaf ad-Dīn ʿAbdu'llāh (A.H. 578–643), the son of Shaikh Abū ʿUmar. Shaikh al-Muwaffaq was the one who used to lead the prayer in the niche of the Ḥanbalīs in the Mosque of Banī Umayya, when he came down from Mount Qāsiyūn to the city of Damascus. While he was on the mountain, the prayer was led by his maternal cousin, ʿImād ad-Dīn Ibrāhīm (A.H. 543–614). After the death of al-ʿImād, the prayer was led by Abū Sulaimān ʿAbd ar-Raḥmān (A.H. 583–643), the son of al-Ḥāfiẓ ʿAbd al-Ghanī, except when al-Muwaffaq was present, for no one took precedence over him in leading the prayer and delivering the sermon.

The literary works of al-Muwaffaq are all magnificent, and his treatises are too numerous to be counted. The most important of his literary works are the following:

1. *al-ʿUmda fi 'l-Fiqh* [The Mainstay, concerning Jurisprudence.] (For beginners.) In this work, the author has confined himself to the doctrine firmly established in the [Ḥanbalī] school of law. He has prefaced every chapter with an authentic Prophetic tradition *[ḥadīth]*, then presented topics which the intelligent reader will find, if he reflects upon them, to be derived from that Prophetic tradition. Because of the precious value and the exactitude of this text, Shaikh al-Islām Ibn Taimiyya undertook its commentary.

The book *al-ʿUdda* [The Equipment], which we are now engaged in printing, is another commentary on it, of extremely precious value, and it predates the commentary of Shaikh al-Islām. Its compiler, al-Bahāʾ ʿAbd ar-Raḥmān ibn Ibrāhīm al-Maqdisī (A.H. 556–624) was a pupil of Imām al-Muwaffaq, who studied jurisprudence under him, and who understood his aims and his goals.

2. *al-Muqniʿ fi 'l-Fiqh* [The Sufficer, concerning Jurisprudence]. (For students at the middle stage.) In many of the topics of this work, the author cites two traditional reports, for the purpose of training the student in the evaluation of the reports. The student is thereby trained to incline toward the proof. The text of *al-Muqniʿ* is now being printed by our press for the second time, in three volumes, at the charitable expense of His Highness Shaikh ʿAlī, the second son of Shaikh ʿAbdu'llāh, the governor of the glorious country. It is being printed together with its marginal commentary, which is thought to be part of the literary work of Shaikh Sulaimān, the son of Shaikh ʿAbdu'llāh, the son of Shaikh Muḥammad ibn ʿAbd al-Wahhāb (may Allāh bestow His mercy upon them). Because of the importance of the book *al-Muqniʿ* for the accurate recording of the *[Ḥanbalī]* doctrine, the eminent al-Mardāwī revised it in his book *al-Inṣāf* [Equity] and its synopsis *at-Tanqīḥ al-Mushabbaʿ* [The Full Revision]. It was also summarized by Shaikh Sharaf ad-Dīn Abu 'n-Najā al-Ḥajāwī, who died in the year A.H. 968, in his book *Zād al-Mustaqniʿ* [Sufficient Provision for the Seeker of Satisfaction], which was commented upon by Shaikh Manṣūr ibn Yūnus al-Bahūtī, who died in the year A.H. 1051, in his book *ar-Rawḍ al-Murbiʿ* [The Fertile Meadow]. Both *Zād al-Mustaqniʿ* and its commentary *ar-Rawḍ al-Murbiʿ* have been printed more than once by our press.
3. *al-Kāfī fi 'l-Fiqh* [The Fully Sufficient, concerning Jurisprudence.] (More comprehensive than *al-Kāfī*.) In this work, the author furnishes proofs to equip the students for action based on proof.
4. *al-Mughnī fi 'l-Fiqh* [The Enricher, concerning Jurisprudence], consisting of ten parts. (Commentary on the *Mukhtaṣār* of al-Kharaqī). In this work, the author mentions the various schools of law and

their proofs. If the serious student of jurisprudence reflects on it with care, and if he possesses an aptitude for independent judgment *[ijtihād]*, he will understand its methods. To quote the words of al-ʿIzz ibn ʿAbd as-Salām: "In all the books of Islām concerning religious knowledge, I have never seen the like of *al-Muḥallā* by Ibn Ḥazm and the book *al-Mughnī* by [al-Muwaffaq] Ibn Qudāma, in view of their excellence and the accuracy of their contents." He also said: "I never felt comfortable about delivering a formal legal opinion, until I had a copy of *al-Mughnī* at my disposal." As for al-Kharaqī, the author of *al-Mukhtaṣār*, he is Abu 'l-Qāsim ʿUmar ibn al-Ḥasan ibn ʿAbdi'llāh al-Baghdādī, who died in Damascus in the year A.H. 334.

5. Synopsis of *al-Hidāya* [Guidance] by Abu 'l-Khaṭṭāb ibn Aḥmad ibn al-Ḥasan al-Kalūdhānī al-Baghdādī (A.H. 432–510), the author of *al-Qaṣīda ad-Dāliyya* [the Ode Rhyming in "-d"] on the Sunna, who was one of the Shaikhs of Shaikh ʿAbd al-Qādir al-Jīlānī, the Shaikh of Shaikh al-Muwaffaq.
6. *Rawḍat an-Nāẓir fī Uṣūl al-Fiqh* [Garden of the Student of the Sources of Jurisprudence]. We published it in print in the year A.H. 1342, at the command of King ʿAbd al-ʿAzīz of the dynasty of Saʿūd (may Allāh bestow His mercy upon him), together with its commentary entitled *Nuzhat al-Khāṭir al-ʿĀṭir* [Recreation Park of the Fragrant Mind] by Shaikh ʿAbd al-Qādir Badrān al-Dimashqī, who died in the year A.H. 1346. (Two volumes.)
7. Synopsis of *ʿIlal al-Ḥadīth* [The Occasions of the Prophetic Tradition] by Abū Bakr Aḥmad ibn Muḥammad ibn Hārūn al-Khallāl, who died in the year A.H. 311. (Published in a single thick volume, although the original consists of a number of manuscript tomes.)
8. *Mukhtaṣar fī Gharīb al-Ḥadīth* [Synopsis of the Strange Elements of the Prophetic Tradition].
9. *Qunʿat al-Arīb fi 'l-Gharīb* [The Mendicity of the Expert in the Extraordinary].
10. *al-Burhān fī Masʾalat al-Qurʾān* [The Proof concerning the Question of the Qurʾān].
11. *Jawāb Masʾala Waradat min Ṣarkhad fi 'l-Qurʾān* [The Answer to a Question Raised by Ṣarkhad concerning the Qurʾān.]

12. *Mas'alat al-ʿUluww* [The Question of Sublimity]. (Two parts.)
13. *Kitāb at-Tawwābīn* [The Book of the Penitents]. (Concerning the Prophetic Tradition. Two parts.)
14. *Kitāb al-Qadar* [The Book of Destiny]. (Two parts.)
15. *Faḍā'il aṣ-Ṣaḥāba* [The Virtues of the Companions]. (This may be the same as *Minhāj al-Qāṣidīn fī Faḍā'il al-Khulafā' ar-Rāshidīn* [The Path of the Emulators of the Virtues of the Rightly Guided Caliphs]).
16. *Kitāb al-Mutaḥābbīna fi 'llāh* [The Book of those who Love One Another for Allāh's Sake].
17. *Kitāb ar-Riqqa wa 'l-Bukā'* [The Book of Sensitivity and Weeping]. (Two parts.)
18. *at-Tabyīn fī Nasab al-Qurashiyyīn* [Explanation of the Genealogy of the Members of the Tribe of Quraish]. (Published by the Egyptian Library).
19. *al-Istibṣār fī Nasab al-Anṣār* [Consideration of the Genealogy of the Helpers]. (Published by the Egyptian Library).
20. *Risāla ila 'sh-Shaikh Fakhr ad-Dīn ibn Taimiyya fī Takhlīd Ahl al-Bidaʿ fi 'n-Nār* [A Treatise addressed to Shaikh Fakhr ad-Dīn ibn Taimiyya concerning the Consignment of the Heretical Innovators to Eternal Damnation in the Fire of Hell].
21. *Mas'ala fī Taḥrīm an-Naẓar fī Kutub Ahl al-Kalām* [A Question about the Prohibition of Studying the Books of the Theologians].
22. *Lumʿa fi 'l-Iʿtiqād* [A Ray of Light on Religious Belief].
23. *Dhamm at-Ta'wīl* [Criticism of Interpretation]. (Printed in *Majmūʿat ar-Radd al-Wāfir* [The Compendium of Abundant Refutation], and subsequently reprinted.)
24. *Muqaddima fi 'l-Farā'iḍ* [Introduction to the Obligatory Religious Duties].
25. *Manāsik al-Ḥajj* [The Rites of Pilgrimage].
26. *Dhamm al-Muwaswisīn* [Criticism of the Tempters]. (Printed in *Majmūʿat ar-Rasā'il al-Munīriyya* [The Compendium of Enlightening Treatises]).
27. *Kitāb Ṣifat al-Falaq* [The Book of the Nature of the Dawn].
28. *Faḍā'il ʿĀshūrā'* [The Excellent Qualities of the Day of ʿĀshūrā'].
29. *Faḍā'il al-ʿAshr* [The Excellent Qualities of the First Ten Days of Muḥarram].

30. *Majmūʿa Fatāwā* [Collection of Formal Legal Opinions].
31–32. Books about the Shaikhs of his Shaikhs, and other Shaikhs. (Many parts.)

The Ḥassān of the seventh century of the Hijra,[1] Jamāl ad-Dīn Abū Zakariyyā Yaḥyā ibn Yūsuf al-Anṣārī aṣ-Ṣarṣarī (A.H. 588–656), is the author of a magnificent ode rhyming in "-l", in which he extols Shaikh al-Muwaffaq and his books. It includes these verses:

In our generation al-Muwaffaq was an authority
whose jurisprudence was firmly based on the roots.
He satisfied people with *al-Kāfī* and, with *al-Muqniʿ*,
gave a student sufficient to learn without a lengthy book.
With *al-Mughnī* he enriched the inquiring scholar,
and anyone supported by *al-ʿUmda* will surely succeed.
His *Rawḍa* contains the roots, like a garden
where the flowers are swayed by the breaths of a breeze.
It provides the legal text with perfect proof,
and conveys the meaning with excellent explanation.

Imām al-Muwaffaq has much fine poetry of his own, and he is said to be the author of an ode in the kind of language that is very abstruse [*ʿawīṣ al-lugha*]. His poetry includes the following verses:

You must not sit at the door of anyone
who refuses you admittance to his house.
When you say: "I am in need of it,"
he obstructs your need if he does not swing the door.
You must leave him and seek the Owner of the house,
lest you die while the Owner is displeased.
The cups of death are circling around us,
and each man is bound to receive a share.
How long will you make a habit of procrastination?
Are you not satisfied with the warning of graying hair?
Is it not enough for you that every moment
passes without a bosom friend or loved one?
It seems that you had contact with them recently,
and no excess of lamentation is enough for you.

The grandson of Ibn al-Jawzī said: "Al-Muwaffaq recited these verses to me:

Shall I keep my hair from turning white? Shall I live as if
the grave does not exist? If I do so, what a fool am I!

[1] The Ḥassān of the first century was Ḥassān ibn Thābit, an Arab poet who embraced Islām and became a Companion and eulogist of the Prophet (Allāh bless him and give him peace).

Each day and each night is tearing my life to shreds,
so is anyone capable of mending what is torn to shreds?
I seem to be with my body stretched out on my bier,
so it is scorched by either a silent or a wailing mourner.
A most trustworthy friend is scattering the earth upon me,
and one who is compassionate is committing me to the grave.
O Lord, be a close companion for me on the day of my loneliness,
for I am truly a believer in what You have revealed!"

Imām al-Muwaffaq was transported to Allāh's mercy and the abundance of His grace on Saturday, the day of the Festival of Breaking Fast *[ʿĪd al-Fiṭr]* in the year A.H. 620, and the funeral prayer was performed for him on the following day. He was carried to the foothill of Mount Qāsiyūn in the Ṣalāḥiyya district of Damascus, and there he was buried above the congregational mosque of the Ḥanbalīs, to the north, beneath the cavern known as the Cavern of Repentance. May Allāh bestow His mercy upon him, and may He cause his Afterlife to be lived in the company of the righteous, who dwell for all eternity in everlasting bliss!

Author's Introduction

In the Name of Allāh, the All-Merciful, the All-Compassionate

[Bismi'llāhi 'r-Raḥmāni 'r-Raḥīm]

Praise be to Allāh, who is worthy of praise and deserving thereof—a praise that excels all praise, like the excellence of Allāh over His creation. I bear witness that there is no god but Allāh, Alone without any partner, thereby fulfilling for Allāh His rightful due. I also bear witness that Muḥammad is His servant and His Messenger, having no doubt as to his truthfulness. May Allāh bestow blessing and peace upon him, and upon his family and his Companions, as often as the clouds bring pouring rain, and as often as thunder follows the lightning flash.

This is a book concerning jurisprudence *[fiqh]*. I have made it as concise as possible, and in it I have confined myself to a single doctrine, so that it may be a mainstay *[ʿumda]* for its reader. The correct view is thus unobscured by difference of approaches and accounts.

One of my brethren asked me to condense it, so that it would be convenient for the scholars, and easy for the students to memorize. I have therefore responded to his request, relying upon Allāh (Glory be to Him) for sincerity in seeking His generous favor, and for help in attaining to His glorious approval. He is all that we need, and Most Excellent is the Custodian!

I have supplied it with authentic Prophetic traditions *[aḥādīth ṣaḥīḥa]*, for the sake of the blessing and support they provide, and I have taken them from the authentic collections, in order to do without citing their chains of transmission.

The Book of Ritual Purification

Chapter

The Legal Rules concerning Types of Water *[Aḥkām al-Miyāh]*

Water was created pure. It is the means of purification from excrements *[aḥdāth]* and other kinds of filth *[najāsāt]*. The state of ritual purity *[ṭahāra]* is not achieved by means of any other liquid. If the water amounts to nothing less than the contents of two large vessels *[qullatān]*, or if it is flowing, nothing will pollute it, except that which changes its color, or its taste, or its smell. Anything apart from that is polluted by the admixture of the impurity. The term *qullatān* refers to a quantity approximately equal to one hundred and eighty rotls in the Syrian system of weights.[2]

If something that is not pure is cooked in the water, and likewise if something mingles with it to the point where it robs it of its name, or if it is used for the purpose of removing excrement, it is deprived of its natural purity.

If a person has any misgiving about the purity of the water—or anything else—and its uncleanness, he should base his action on what he knows for certain. If it is unclear whether the impurity is situated on his clothing or elsewhere, he should wash whatever he feels sure about washing. If some pure water is hard to distinguish from some that is polluted, and he cannot find any other, he should perform the dry ablution *[tayammum]*[3] and abandon them both. If some that is extremely pure *[ṭahūr]* is hard to distinguish from some

[2] The English word "rotl" is derived from the Arabic *raṭl*. Its weight, which varies from country to country, is said to be about four pounds in Syria.

[3] The dry ablution *[tayammum]* is performed by patting the hands on the dusty surface of a clean patch of earth, then rubbing the appropriate parts of the body.

that is merely clean *[ṭāhir]*, he should perform the minor ritual ablution *[wuḍū']* by using both of them. If the garments that are clean are hard to distinguish from those that are dirty, he should perform a ritual prayer *[ṣalāt]* in each garment, according to the number of those that are dirty, and add another ritual prayer.

The filth of the dog and the swine should be ritually cleansed seven times, six times with water and one time with dust. Three acts of cleansing are sufficient for other kinds of filth. If the filth is on the ground, one pouring [of water] is enough remove it, because of his saying (Allāh bless him and give him peace):

> Pour on the urine of the Bedouin a bucketful of water.

It is sufficient to sprinkle water on the urine of a youth who has not eaten food, and the same applies to a discharge of prostatic fluid *[madhy]*. A slight trace of this is overlooked, as is a slight trace of blood and any pus or similar matter discharged from it. The expression "slight trace" refers to that which is not soaked in blood. The semen of a human being is pure, and so is the urine of any creature whose flesh may be eaten.

Chapter

Vessels, Receptacles, Containers *[al-Āniya]*

It is not permissible to use vessels of gold and silver, whether in a state of purity or any other condition, because Ḥudhaifa reported that the Prophet (Allāh bless him and give him peace) once said:

> Do not drink from vessels of gold and silver, and do not eat from dishes made of those metals, for they belong to them [the unbelievers] in this world, and to you in the Hereafter.

The same rule applies to the metal band used to repair them, unless it is a tiny piece of silver. It is permissible to make use of all other clean vessels, as well as to use the vessels of the people of the Scripture and their clothes, so long as they are not known to be unclean. The wool of the dead animal is clean, and so is its hair. As for the hide of any dead animal, whether or not it has been tanned, it is unclean. The same applies to its bones. Every corpse is unclean, with the following exceptions: (1) the corpse of the human being, (2) the corpse of the aquatic animal that lives only in the water, because of the saying of Allāh's Messenger (Allāh bless him and give him peace) concerning the ocean:

> It is that of which the water is pure, and of which the corpse is lawful food.

(3) the corpse of a creature that has no flowing blood, so long as it is not generated from impure substances.

Chapter

Fulfillment of the Need to Answer the Call of Nature *[Qaḍā' al-Ḥāja]*

When someone is about to enter the toilet, it is commendable for him to say:

In the Name of Allāh.	*Bismi'llāh.*
I take refuge with Allāh from wickedness and wicked deeds,	*a'ūdhu bi'llāhi mina 'l-khubuthi wa 'l-khabā'ith:*
and from the foul one, the filthy one, Satan the accursed.	*wa mina 'r-rajisi 'n-najisi ' sh-Shaiṭāni 'r-rajim.*

When he comes out, he should say:

I beg Your forgiveness.	*ghufrāna-k.*
Praise be to Allāh, who has relieved me of trouble and kept me healthy.	*al-ḥamdu li'llāhi 'lladhī adhhaba 'an-ni 'l-adhā wa 'āfā-nī.*

He should put his left foot forward on entering, and his right foot on coming out. He should not enter the toilet with anything in which Allāh (Exalted is He) is mentioned, except in urgent need. In his sitting posture, he should rest his weight on his left foot. If he is in open country, he should move far away, keep himself out of sight, and look for a soft spot that will absorb his urine. He should not urinate in a hole, nor a crevice, nor on a path, nor in a useful shade, nor beneath a tree bearing fruit. He must not face toward the sun or the moon, and he must turn neither his face nor his back toward the Qibla [direction of prayer], because of the saying of Allāh's Messenger (Allāh bless him and give him peace):

> Do not turn your faces toward the Qibla when defecating or urinating, and do not turn your backs toward it.

That is permissible inside a building, however, [when the Qibla is unclear].

As soon as he has finished urinating, he should rub his penis from its root to its tip, then shake it hard three times. He should not touch his penis with his right hand, nor should he rub with it. Next, he should perform *istijmār* [cleansing with pebbles] an odd number of times, followed by *istinjā'* [cleansing with water]. If he confines himself to *istijmār*, that is sufficient, but only if what is excreted does not spread beyond the orifice. Fewer than three cleansing wipes are insufficient. It is permissible to perform *istijmār* with any clean substance, and so become purified, except *rawth* [the dung of a solid-hoofed animal], bones, and anything that is sacrosanct.

Chapter

The Minor Ritual Ablution *[Wuḍū']*

The minor ritual ablution *[wuḍū']* is not valid, and neither is any other act of worship, unless its practitioner begins by formulating his intention to perform it, because of the saying of Allāh's Messenger (Allāh bless him and give him peace):

> Actions are valued only by the intentions [on the strength of which they are performed], and every man is credited with what he actually intended.

Having formulated his intention, he should proceed as follows:

- He should say: "In the Name of Allāh *[Bismi'llāh]*."
- He should wash the palms of his hands three times.
- He should rinse his mouth and his nostrils three times, using one or three scoops of water in the process.
- He should wash his face three times, lengthwise from the points where hair grows on the head down to the curve of the jawbones, and breadthwise from ear to ear. He should run his wet fingers through his beard, if it is thick, but if it is merely stubble on the skin he is obliged to wash it.
- He should wash his hands [and his lower arms] up to the elbows, three times, and dip them into the washbowl.
- He should rub his head, including both ears. He should begin by placing his hands on his forehead, then draw them across to the nape of his neck, and then bring them back to his forehead.
- He should wash his feet up to the ankles, three times, and dip them into the washbowl. He should also run his wet fingers between the toes.
- He should turn his gaze up toward the sky, and say:

I bear witness that there is no god but Allāh,	*ashhadu al-lā ilāha illa 'llāhu*
Alone without any partner.	*Waḥda-hu lā sharīka la-h.*
I also bear witness that Muḥammad	*wa ashhadu anna Muḥammadan*
is His servant and His Messenger.	*'abdu-hu wa Rasūlu-h.*

Among the elements listed above, the following: are strictly obligatory:

- The intention *[niyya]*.
- Washing one time in each case, with the exception of the palms of the hand.
- Rubbing the whole of the head.
- Performing the ablution in the correct sequence, as we have described.
- The washing of a member of the body must not be delayed until the one before it becomes dry.

The following elements are customary *[masnūn]* :

- The invocation of Allāh's Name *[at-tasmiya]*.
- Exaggeration in the rinsing of the mouth and nostrils, except in the case of someone who is fasting.
- Running the fingers through the beard and between the fingers and toes.
- Rubbing the ears.
- Washing the parts on the right side before those on the left side.
- Washing three times in each case.

Washing more than three times is disapproved, and so is the extravagant use of water.

It is customary to use the toothpick *[siwāk]* whenever the mouth is tainted, when arising from sleep, and at the time of ritual prayer, because of the saying of Allāh's Messenger (Allāh bless him and give him peace):

> If I could have done so without imposing hardship on my Community, I would have commanded them to use the toothpick at the time of every prayer.

It is also recommended at other times, except for the person who is fasting in the afternoon.

Chapter

Wiping the Shoes
[Masḥ al-Khuffain]

[Instead of washing the feet] it is permissible to wipe over the shoes, or similar articles of footwear, and galoshes that extend above the ankles, in order to maintain the state of minor purity between one cause of major impurity and another—for one day and night in the case of the resident, and three in the case of the traveler, because of the saying of Allāh's Messenger (Allāh bless him and give him peace):

> The traveler may practice wiping for three days and nights, and the resident for one day and night.

When he practices wiping, but then the period expires—or he undresses before it does so—his state of purity is annulled. If someone practices wiping as a traveler, but then settles down—or as a resident, but then embarks on a journey—he may complete the period of wiping permitted to a resident.

[Instead of rubbing the head], it is permissible to wipe over the turban, provided it has a fringe that covers the whole of the head, apart from what is usually exposed to view.

In every case, wiping over the article of clothing is permissible only on condition that he dons it while in a state of perfect purity.

It is also permissible to wipe over a surgical splint *[jabīra]*, if he does not dislodge it from its proper position until he unfastens it.

The same rules apply to the man and the woman, except that the woman may not wipe over the turban.

Chapter

Factors that Annul the Minor Ritual Ablution *[Nawāqiḍ al-Wuḍū᾿]*

These are seven in number:

1. What is excreted from the two orifices.
2. The dirt excreted from the rest of the body, if it is indecent.
3. The loss of mental consciousness, except for a little nap while sitting or standing.
4. Touching the penis with one's hand.
5. Making skin-contact with the skin of a female for the sake of carnal desire.
6. Apostasy from Islām.
7. Eating the flesh of the pig, because of the following traditional report: The Prophet (Allāh bless him and give him peace) was asked: "Must we purify ourselves from the flesh of slaughtered camels by performing the minor ablution?" He said: "Yes, you must purify yourselves from it by performing the minor." He was then asked: "Must we perform the minor ablution to purify ourselves from the flesh of sheep and goats?" To this he replied: "If you wish, perform the minor ablution, and if you do not wish, do not perform it."

If someone is convinced of the state of purity, but in doubt as to the cause of impurity, or he is convinced of the cause of impurity, but in doubt as to the state of purity, he is obliged to accept the alternative of which he is convinced.

Chapter

The Major Ritual Ablution
[al-Ghusl mina 'l-Janāba]

This is necessitated by the emission of sperm, which is the seminal fluid, and by contact with circumcisers.

Its obligatory elements are:

- Formulating the intention *[niyya]*.
- The washing of the entire body, including *maḍmaḍa* [rinsing out the mouth] and *istinshāq* [snuffing water up the nostrils].

Its customary elements are:

- Invoking the Name of Allāh *[at-tasmiya]*.
- Rubbing the body with both hands.
- Acting in accordance with the traditional report of Maimūna, who said: "I screened the Prophet (Allāh bless him and give him peace) while he performed the major ablution. He began by washing his hands, then poured water over his left side with his right hand. He washed his pudendum and the parts close to it. Then he struck with his hand on the wall and on the ground. Then he performed his minor ablution *[wuḍū']* for the ritual prayer. Then he poured water over his body. Then he leaned back and washed his feet."

It is not necessary to unravel the hair during the major ablution, provided one wets its roots.

If someone performs his washing with the intention of acquiring both states of ritual purity [minor and major], that is sufficient for them both. By the same token, if he performs the dry ablution *[tayammum]* with the intention of purifying the two excrements and the dirt on his body, that is sufficient for the whole. If he intends only part of it, however, he is credited only with what he intended.

Chapter

The Dry Ablution
[Tayammum]

This is performed in the following manner: The person concerned strikes with his hands on a clean piece of ground, striking one time only, then rubs them over his face and his palms, because the Prophet (Allāh bless him and give him peace) once said to 'Ammār:

> The only way for you to do it properly is like this—and he struck the earth with his hands, then rubbed them over his face and his palms.

If someone performs the dry ablution with more than one strike, or more than one rubbing, that is permissible.

In order to perform the dry ablution, he must satisfy four preconditions:

1. The unfeasibility of using water, because of its absence; or because its use might be harmful due to sickness or extreme cold; or for fear of inflicting thirst on himself, his companion or his beast; or because the search for it would put himself or his property in danger; or because it is unavailable except at a very high price. If it is possible for him to use it for part of his body, or he finds a quantity of water that is not sufficient for his ritual purification, he should use it and apply the dry ablution to the rest.
2. The arrival of the prescribed time. He must not perform the dry ablution for an obligatory prayer *[farīḍa]* before its prescribed time, nor for a supererogatory prayer *[nāfila]* at the time of its prohibition.
3. The intention *[niyya]*. If he performs the dry ablution for a supererogatory prayer, he may not perform an obligatory prayer on the strength of it. If he performs the dry ablution for an obligatory prayer, he may perform that prayer, and he may perform whatever

obligatory and supererogatory prayers he wishes, until their time expires.

4. Using the proper kind of earth. He may not perform the dry ablution except with clean earth that is dusty.

The dry ablution is annulled by anything that annuls the purity of water, by the expiration of the prescribed time, and by the feasibility of using water, even if it only becomes available during the ritual prayer.

Chapter

Menstruation
[Ḥaiḍ]

Menstruation prevents ten things:

1. The performance of the ritual prayer.
2. The obligation to perform the ritual prayer.
3. The keeping of the fast.
4. The circumambulation [of the Kaʿba].
5. The reading of the Qurʾān.
6. Touching the volume [of the Qurʾān].
7. Staying in the mosque.
8. Penetration of the vulva.
9. The customary practice of divorce by repudiation *[ṭalāq]*.
10. The reckoning of the months of the *ʿidda* [period of waiting before remarriage is permissible].

It necessitates the major ablution, the attainment of maturity, and keeping account of its duration. When the bleeding stops, the keeping of the fast becomes permissible, and so does divorce by repudiation, but the other practices [listed above] do not become permissible until the woman performs the major ablution.

It is permissible [for the husband] to enjoy physical contact with the menstruating woman, excluding her vagina, because of the saying of the Prophet (Allāh bless him and give him peace):

> Do anything other than copulate.

The shortest period of menstruation is a day and a night, while the longest is fifteen days. The shortest interval of purity between two menstrual periods is thirteen days, and there is no limit to its longest interval. The earliest age at which a woman menstruates is nine years, and the latest is sixty. When the beginner notices bleeding at a time when she is likely to menstruate, she must sit down. Then, if the bleeding stops in less than a day and a night, it is not a menstruation. If it continues beyond that, and most of the emission has not passed through, it is a menstruation. If it recurs for three months in a single manner, it has become a habit. If most of the emission has passed through, the excess is an *istiḥaḍa* [non-menstrual bleeding from the vagina].

She is obliged to perform the major ablution at the end of the menstruation. As for *istiḥaḍa*, it is classed among the states of purity with regard to the obligatory nature of worship and its performance. When she intends to perform the ritual prayer, she must therefore wash her vagina and bandage it. She must then perform the minor ablution at the time of each ritual prayer, and proceed to pray. The same rule applies to someone who suffers from incontinence of the bladder and any similar condition.

If her bleeding continues into the next month, and if this is a regular occurrence, her menstrual period consists of the days of her usual experience. If it is not a regular occurrence, however, and a distinction is noticeable in her bleeding—namely, that some of her blood is black and thick, while some of it is red and thin—her menstrual period is the time of the thick black bleeding. If she is a beginner, or oblivious of her usual experience, and there is no distinction in her bleeding, her menstrual period is six or seven days of each month, because that is the normal experience of women.

The pregnant woman does not menstruate, except that she may see herself bleeding for one, two or three days before giving birth, in which case it is the blood of postnatal effusion *[nifās]*.

Chapter

Postnatal Effusion
[Nifās]

This is the bleeding that occurs as a result of giving birth. Its legal status is that of menstruation, with regard to what it renders lawful and unlawful, and what is necessary and unnecessary because of it. Its maximum duration is forty days, but there is no limit to its minimum. When she sees that she is clear of bleeding, she must perform the major ablution and so become ritually pure. If the bleeding recurs during the period of forty days, it also constitutes postnatal effusion.

The Book of the Ritual Prayer
[Kitāb aṣ-Ṣalāt]

The Book of the Ritual Prayer
[Kitāb aṣ-Ṣalāt]

'Ubāda ibn aṣ-Ṣāmit (may Allāh be well pleased with him) is reported as having said: "I once heard Allāh's Messenger (Allāh bless him and give him peace) say:

> There are five ritual prayers which Allāh has prescribed for His servants in the course of the day and the night. If someone is careful to observe them, he has a covenant with Allāh that He will allow him to enter the Garden of Paradise. If someone is not careful to observe them, he has no covenant with Allāh. If He so wills, He will punish him, and if He so wills, He will forgive him.

The five ritual prayers are therefore obligatory for every adult Muslim of sound mind, except those women who are menstruating and those have recently given birth. If someone denies their obligatory nature because of his ignorance, he must be informed thereof. If he denies it willfully, he is guilty of unbelief. It is not lawful to postpone them beyond the time prescribed for their performance, except in the case of someone who intends to combine them, or who is engaged in fulfilling their precondition. If he fails to perform them because he regards them with disdain, he must be called upon three times to repent. If he does repent, well and good, but if not, he should be killed.

Chapter

The Call to Prayer
[Adhān]
and the Announcement that Prayer is About to Begin
[Istiqāma]

These are both prescribed by Islāmic law for the five [obligatory] ritual prayers, to the exclusion of others, and for men to the exclusion of women. The call to prayer *[adhān]* consists of fifteen sentences, with no *tarjī'* [repetition of each section in a louder tone of voice]. The announcement that prayer is about to begin *[istiqāma]* consists of eleven sentences.

The man who gives the call [the *mu'adhdhin*, or "muezzin" in English usage] must be trustworthy, of good repute, thoroughly acquainted with the times of prayer.

It is recommended that he give the call while standing, in a state of ritual purity, on a high place, facing the *Qibla*.

When he reaches the *ḥai'ala* [the expression "Come to the prayer (*ḥayya 'ala 'ṣ-ṣalāh*)!"], he should turn to the right and to the left, without shifting his feet, and he should place his thumbs in his ears.

He should proceed at a leisurely pace in the *adhān*, and rapidly in the *istiqāma*.

In the call to early morning prayer *[adhān aṣ-ṣubḥ]*, he should declare two times after the *ḥai'ala* :

Prayer is better than sleep!	*aṣ-ṣalātu khairun mina 'n-nawm*

He should not give the call before the times of prayer, except [in preparation] for them, because of the saying Allāh's Messenger (Allāh bless him and give him peace):

> Bilāl gives the call to prayer at night, so eat and drink until Ibn Umm Maktūm gives the call.

When someone hears the muezzin, it is commendable for him to repeat his words, because of the saying Allāh's Messenger (Allāh bless him and give him peace):

> When you hear the summons, say the same words as he is saying.

Chapter

The Prerequisites of the Ritual Prayer *[Shurūṭ as-Ṣalāt]*

These are six in number:

1. The state of purity from excrement, because of the saying Allāh's Messenger (Allāh bless him and give him peace):

   > There is no ritual prayer for someone who has excreted, until he performs the minor ablution.

2. The prescribed time. The time of the midday prayer *[ẓuhr]* lasts from the sun's decline from the meridian, until the moment when the shadow cast by each thing becomes equal to it in length. The time of the afternoon prayer *[ʿaṣr]*—which is the middle [of the five prayers]—lasts from the time of the midday prayer until the sun turns yellow. The time of free choice then expires, and the time of urgency remains until the setting of the sun. The time of the sunset prayer *[maghrib]* lasts until the red glow of twilight disappears. The time of the late evening prayer *[ʿishāʾ]* lasts from that moment until the middle of the night, then the time of urgency remains until the rising of the second dawn. The time of the dawn prayer *[fajr]* lasts from then until the rising of the sun.
   If someone pronounces the *takbīr* [declaration of the Supreme Greatness of Allāh] for the ritual prayer, before the expiration of its prescribed time, he has caught it before it is too late.
   It is more meritorious to perform the ritual prayer at the beginning of the prescribed time, except in the case of the late evening prayer, and that of the midday prayer when the heat is intense.

3. Covering the private parts with something that does not reveal the skin. The private parts of the man, and of the female slave, consist of the area between the navel and the knee. The entire body of the free woman is private, except her face and the palms of her hands. The [slave woman who is] the mother of the child [of her master] is like the ordinary female slave, and so is one who is partially emancipated.

   If someone performs the ritual prayer in misappropriated clothing, or in a misappropriated dwelling, his prayer is not valid. The wearing of gold and silk is permissible for women, but not for men except in case of need, because of the saying of Allāh's Messenger (Allāh bless him and give him peace) concerning gold and silk:

   > Both of these are unlawful for the males of my Community, lawful for their females.

   If one of the men performs the ritual prayer in a single article of clothing, part of which is draped over his shoulder, that is sufficient for him. If he cannot find anything more than enough to cover his private parts, he should cover them. If he cannot cover them completely, he must conceal his two pudenda. If he cannot cover them both, he must cover one of them. If covering is absent altogether, he should pray in a sitting position, nodding to indicate the acts of bowing *[rukūʿ]* and prostration *[sujūd]*, but it is also permissible for him to pray is an upright posture. If someone can find nothing but a dirty garment, or a dirty place, he should pray in them, and he is not required to repeat the prayer.
4. Purity from dirt on his body, his clothing and the place of his ritual prayer, except the kind of dirt that is excused, such as slight traces of blood and the like. If he performs the prayer when some dirt is upon him, but he is unaware of it, or he knew it was there but then forgot about it, his prayer is valid. If he becomes aware of it during the prayer, he must remove it and carry on with his prayer. The whole earth is a mosque in which the ritual prayer is valid, except the graveyard, the public steam bath, the dunghill, the resting place of camels, and the middle of the road.
5. Facing toward the *Qibla* [direction of the Kaʿba in Mecca], except in the case of the supererogatory prayer performed by the traveler

on a riding animal, for he may pray in whatever direction he is facing, and in the case of someone who dare not turn toward the *Qibla* because of some danger, for he may pray however he can. With these two exceptions, no one's ritual prayer is valid unless he is facing toward the Kaʿba. If he is close to it, he is obliged to perform the prayer toward the building itself, and if he is far away, in its direction. If the *Qibla* is unclear in a settled area, he should make inquiries and seek guidance from the prayer niches of the Muslims. If he makes a mistake, he is obliged to repeat the prayer. If the *Qibla* is unclear on a journey, he should exercise his own judgment and perform the prayer accordingly, and no repetition is then required of him. If two experts differ in their judgment, one of them should not follow his companion, and the blind man and the commoner should follow whichever of the two experts is more self-confident.

6. The intention to perform the particular ritual prayer. It is permissible to formulate the intention in advance of the *takbīr* [declaration of the Supreme Greatness of Allāh], by a brief interval of time, provided that one does nothing to abrogate it.

Chapter

The Proprieties of Walking to the Ritual Prayer *[Ādāb al-Mashy ila 's-Ṣalāt]*

When someone is walking to the ritual prayer, it is commendable for him to be in a state of calm and dignified composure, to take short steps, and to refrain from twisting his fingers. He should say: "In the Name of Allāh *[Bismi'llāh]*," then recite these Qur'ānic verses:

The One who created me, and Himself guides me, and Himself gives me to eat and drink, and, whenever I am sick, heals me, and who causes me to die, then brings me back to life, and who, I ardently hope, will forgive me my sin on the Day of Doom.	*alladhī khalaqa-nī* *fa-Huwa yahdīn:* *wa 'lladhī Huwa yuṭ* *'imu-nī wa yasqīn:* *wa idhā mariḍtu* *fa-Huwa yashfīn:* *wa 'lladhī yumītu-nī* *thumma yuḥyī-n:* *wa 'lladhī aṭma'u an yaghfira* *lī khaṭī'atī yawma 'd-dīn.*
My Lord, grant me wisdom and unite me with the righteous, and give me a good report in the later generations, and place me among the inheritors of the Garden of Delight, and forgive my father. He is one of those who err,	*Rabbi hab lī ḥukman* *wa alḥiq-nī bi'ṣ-ṣāliḥīn:* *wa 'j'al lī lisāna ṣidqin* *fi 'l-ākhirīn:* *wa 'j'al-nī min warathati* *jannati 'n-na'īm:* *wa 'ghfir li-abī inna-hu kāna* *mina 'ẓ-ẓālimīn:*
And do not abase me on the day when they are raised, the day when neither wealth nor sons will avail [any man], except one who comes to Allāh with a whole heart.	*wa lā tukhzi-nī* *yawma yub'athūn:* *yawma lā yanfa'u mālun* *wa lā banūn:* *illā man ata 'llāha* *bi-qalbin salīm.* (26:78–89)

He should also say:

> O Allāh, I beg You with the rightful claim all beggars have on You,
> and with the rightful claim of one who walks this way,
> for I have not been guilty of any impertinence,
> nor any wantonness, nor any ostentation, nor any notoriety.
> I have come forth wary of Your displeasure
> and eager for Your approval.
> I beg You to deliver me from the Fire of Hell,
> and to forgive me my sins,
> for surely no one forgives sins except You!

When he hears the *iqāma* [announcement that the prayer is about to begin], he should not run toward it, because of the saying of Allāh's Messenger (Allāh bless him and give him peace):

> When the ritual prayer is announced, do not come to it running in haste. Come to it in a state of calm composure. Perform as much of the prayer as you have arrived in time to perform, and then complete whatever you have missed.

Once the prayer has been announced, there is no time to perform any prayer except the one prescribed.

When someone reaches the mosque, he should enter with his right foot first, and say:

In the Name of Allāh,	*Bismi'llāh:*
and blessing and peace	*wa 'ṣ-ṣalātu wa 's-salāmu*
be upon Allāh's Messenger.	*ʿalā Rasūli 'llāh.*
O Allāh, forgive me my sins,	*Allāhumma 'ghfir lī dhunūbī*
and open for me the doors	*wa 'ftaḥ lī abwāba raḥmati-k.*
of Your mercy!	

When he leaves the mosque, he should step out with his left foot first, and repeat those words, except that he should say:

and open for me the doors	*wa 'ftaḥ lī abwāba faḍli-k.*
of Your gracious favor!	

Chapter 14

Description of the Ritual Prayer *[Ṣifat as-Ṣalāt]*

When the worshipper stands ready to perform the ritual prayer, he should say:

Allāhu Akbar [Allāh is Supremely Great!]

The prayer leader *[imām]* must pronounce this, and every other *takbīr* [declaration of Allāh's Supreme Greatness], in a loud voice, so that it can be heard by those behind him.

When pronouncing the initial *takbīr*, the worshipper should raise his hands to the level of his shoulders, or to the lobes of his ears. He should then place his hands above his navel, fix his gaze on the place of his prostration *[sujūd]*, and say:

Glory be to You, O Allāh,	*subḥāna-ka 'llāhumma*
and with Your praise!	*wa bi-ḥamdi-ka*
Blessed is Your Name,	*wa tabāraka 'smu-ka*
and Exalted is Your Majesty.	*wa taʿālā jaddu-ka*
There is no god other than You.	*wa lā ilāha ghairu-k.*

Then he should say:

I take refuge with Allāh	*aʿūdhu bi'llāhi mina*
from Satan the accursed.	*'sh-shaiṭāni 'r-rajīm.*

Then he should say:

In the Name of Allāh,	*Bismi'llāhi 'r-Raḥmāni*
the All-Merciful, the	*'r-Raḥīm.*
All-Compassionate.	

He should not pronounce any of that in a loud voice, because of the saying of Anas: "I prayed behind the Prophet (Allāh bless him and give him peace), Abū Bakr, ʿUmar and ʿUthmān, and I did not hear any one of them pronounce '*Bismi'llāhi 'r-Raḥmāni 'r-Raḥīm*' in a loud voice."

Next, he must recite the Opening Sūra of the Qur'ān *[al-Fātiḥa]*. No ritual prayer is credited to someone who fails to recite it, with the exception of the *ma'mūm* [follower of the prayer leader], for the leader's recitation is a recitation on his behalf. He is recommended to recite during the prayer leader's moments of silence, and when his voice is inaudible.

Next, he should recite another Sūra. In the morning prayer, this should be chosen from among the long Sūras in the final section of the Qur'ān; in the sunset prayer, from among the short ones; and in the other prayers, from among those of medium length. The leader should recite in a loud voice in the morning prayer, and in the first two cycles of the sunset prayer and the evening prayer, but his recitation should otherwise be inaudible.

Next, he should pronounce the *takbīr*, while raising his hands as he raised them the first time, then assume the bowing posture *[rukū']* by placing his hands on his knees, spreading his fingers, stretching his back and pointing his head to the front. While holding this posture, he should say, three times:

Glory to my Lord, the Almighty!	*Subḥāna Rabbiya 'l-'Aẓīm.*

He must then raise his head and his hands as before, while saying:

May Allāh hear and accept the praise of one who praises Him!	*Sami'a 'llāhu li-man ḥamida-h.*

Then, while standing in an upright posture, he should say:

Our Lord, and to You be the praise!	*Rabba-nā wa la-ka 'l-ḥamd.*
Enough [praise] to fill the heavens and the earth, and enough to fill anything beyond them, as You wish.	*mil'u 's-samāwāti wa mil'u 'l-arḍ wa mil'u mā shi'ta min shai'in ba'd.*

The follower *[ma'mūm]* should confine himself to the expression:

Our Lord, and to You be the praise!	*Rabba-nā wa la-ka 'l-ḥamd.*

Next, he must pronounce the *takbīr* without raising his hands, and sink to the ground in prostration. The first parts of him to touch the ground should be his knees, then the palms of his hands, then his forehead and his nose. He should keep his upper arms away from his sides, and his stomach from his thighs. He should place his hands opposite his shoulders, and he should be on tiptoe. While holding this posture, he should say, three times:

Glory to my Lord, the Most High!	*Subḥāna Rabbiya 'l-Aʿlā.*

He must then raise his head, while pronouncing the *takbīr*, and sit with his left foot spread horizontally, while placing his right leg so that the right foot is in a perpendicular position [i.e., with the heel raised], and so that his toes are pointing toward the *Qibla* [direction of the Kaʿba]. While sitting in this posture, he should say three times:

My Lord, forgive me!	*Rabbi 'ghfir lī.*

Next, he must perform the act of prostration a second time, in the same manner as the first. Then he must raise his head from the ground, while pronouncing the *takbīr*, stand in an upright posture, and proceed to perform the second cycle of prayer in the same manner as the first. As soon as he has completed both cycles, he must sit with his feet spread horizontally, in order to perform the testimony *[tashahhud]*. He should place his left hand on his left thigh, and his right hand on his right thigh, hold the little finger *[khinṣir]* and the ring finger *[binṣir]* in the grip of his hand, join the thumb *[ibhām]* and the middle finger *[wusṭā]* to form a circle, and point several times with the index finger *[sabbāba]* [of his right hand], while saying:

Greetings, prayers and good deeds are due to Allāh.	*at-taḥiyyātu li'llāhi wa 'ṣ-ṣalawātu wa 'ṭ-ṭayyibāt:*
Peace be upon you, O Prophet, and the mercy of Allāh and His blessings!	*as-salāmu ʿalai-ka ayyuha 'n-Nabiyyu wa raḥmatu'llāhi wa barakātu-h:*
Peace be on us, and on all the righteous servants of Allāh.	*as-salāmu ʿalai-nā wa ʿalā ʿibādi 'llāhi 'ṣ-ṣāliḥīn.*
I bear witness that there is no god but Allāh,	*ashhadu an lā ilāha illa 'llāh:*
and I bear witness that Muḥammad is His servant and His Messenger.	*wa ashhadu anna Muḥammadan ʿabdu-hu wa rasūluh.*

This is the most authentic version of the testimony *[tashahhud]* reported on the authority of the Prophet (Allāh bless him and give him peace).

He must then go on to say:

O Allāh, bless Muḥammad, and the family of Muḥammad, as You have blessed the family of Abraham!	*Allāhumma ṣallī ʿalā Muḥammadin wa ʿalā āli Muḥammad: ka-mā ṣallaita ʿalā āli Ibrāhīm.*
Surely You deserve to be praised and extolled!	*inna-ka Ḥamīdun Majīd.*
And bestow Your grace upon Muḥammad,	*wa bārik ʿalā Muḥammadin*
and upon the family of Muḥammad,	*wa ʿalā āli Muḥammad:*
as You have bestowed Your grace upon the family of Abraham!	*ka-mā bārakta ʿalā āli Ibrāhīm.*
Surely You deserve to be praised and extolled!	*inna-ka Ḥamīdun Majīd.*

It is also recommendable for him to seek refuge from the torment of the tomb and the torment of Hell, from the mischief of life and death, and from the mischief of the False Messiah *[al-Masīḥ ad-Dajjāl]*.

He must then pronounce the *taslīma* [salutation of peace], first to his right and then to his left, by saying:

Peace be upon you, and the Mercy of Allāh!	*as-salāmu ʿalaik-kum wa Raḥmatu 'llāh.*

If the ritual prayer consists of more than two cycles, he must stand up after the first testimony *[tashahhud]*, in the same manner as his standing up from the prostration. He must then perform the remaining cycles without reciting anything in them after the Opening Sūra *[al-Fātiḥa]*.

When he sits for the final testimony *[tashahhud]*, he should adopt the posture called *tawarruk*, by placing his right leg so that his right foot is in a perpendicular position, spreading his left foot horizontally, and causing both feet to protrude from his right side. He should only adopt this posture in a prayer containing two testimonies, and only in the last of the two.

As soon as he has pronounced the salutation of peace, he should seek forgiveness three times, and say:

O Allāh! You are Peace, and from You comes peace! Blessed are You, O Lord of Majesty and Honor!	*Allāhumma Anta 's-Salāmu wa minka 's-salām. tabārakta yā Dha'l-Jalāli wa 'l-Ikrām.*

Chapter

The Basic Essentials of the Ritual Prayer and its Necessary Elements *[Arkān as-Ṣalāt wa Wājibātu-hā]*

Its basic essentials *[arkān]* are twelve in number:

1. Standing in an upright posture *[qiyām]*, provided one is capable thereof.
2. The consecratory affirmation of Allāh's Supreme Greatness *[takbīrat al-iḥrām]*.
3. The recitation of the Opening Sūra of the Qur'ān *[qirā'at al-Fātiḥa]*.
4. The bowing posture *[rukū']*.
5. Straightening up from the bowing posture.
6. The posture of prostration *[sujūd]*.
7. Sitting back from the posture of prostration.
8. Calm composure *[ṭuma'nīna]* in the performance of these basic essentials.
9. The final testimony *[tashahhud]*.
10. Adopting the sitting posture *[julūs]* in order to make the final testimony.
11. The first salutation of peace *[taslīm]*.
12. Their performance in the manner we have described above.
    The ritual prayer is not complete without these essential elements.

Its necessary elements *[wājibāt]* are seven in number:

1. The affirmation of Allāh's Supreme Greatness *[takbīr]*, apart from the consecratory affirmation thereof *[takbīrat al-iḥrām]*.
2. The glorification of the Lord *[tasbīḥ]* each time one adopts the

postures of bowing *[rukūʿ]* and prostration *[sujūd]*.
3. Acknowledging the fact that Allāh hears those who praise Him *[tasmīʿ]*, and then offering praise to Him *[taḥmīd]*, on rising from the bowing posture *[rukūʿ]*.
4. Saying: "*Rabbi 'ghfir lī* [My Lord, forgive me]" between the two acts of prostration.
5. The first testimony *[tashahhud]*.
6. Adopting the sitting posture in order to make the first testimony.
7. The invocation of blessing on the Prophet (Allāh bless him and give him peace) in the final testimony.

If these necessary elements are omitted with deliberate intent, the worshipper's ritual prayer is annulled. If he omits one of them absent-mindedly, he must perform an act of prostration to make up for its omission. Other elements are customary practices *[sunan]*, so the ritual prayer is not annulled by their deliberate omission, and their absent-minded omission does not necessitate prostration.

Chapter

The Two Prostrations for Absent-mindedness *[Sajdatai as-Sahw]*

There are several types of absent-mindedness:

1. Excessive performance of an element of the ritual prayer, such as a cycle *[rakʿa]* or a basic essential *[rukn]*. If this is done deliberately, the ritual prayer is annulled, and prostration is required if it is done absent-mindedly. If the worshipper recovers his memory while he is performing the extra cycle, he must sit down immediately. If he is guilty of no omission in his prayer, he must complete the rest of it and then perform an act of prostration. If he does something that is not an element of the ritual prayer, no distinction is made between deliberate intent and absent-mindedness. What matters is its seriousness, so if it is very serious it annuls the prayer, but if it is trivial—like what the Prophet did (Allāh bless him and give him peace) when he let [his little granddaughter] Umāma sit on his shoulders, and when he opened the door for ʿĀʾisha—no harm is done.
2. Shortcoming like forgetful omission of a necessary element. If the worshipper gets up without performing the first testimony *[tashahhud]*, and then remembers before standing completely upright, he should return [to the sitting posture] and perform it, but if he has adopted the upright posture completely, he should not return. If he forgets a basic essential, and then remembers it before embarking on the Qurʾānic recitation of another cycle, he should return and perform it and what follows it. If he remembers it after that, however, the cycle from which he omitted it is annulled. If he forgets four acts of prostration from four cycles,

and remembers during the testimony *[tashahhud]*, he should prostrate himself immediately, so that one cycle will be valid for him. He must then perform three cycles.

3. Doubt. If someone is in doubt as to whether he has omitted a basic essential, it is just as if he has definitely omitted it. If someone is dubious about the number of cycles, he should act on the basis of what he knows for certain, except in the case of the prayer leader, for he should act on the basis of what he considers most probable.

For every absence of mind, two prostrations must be performed before the salutation of peace, except by someone who feels quite sure that he has not has omitted anything during his prayer, by the prayer leader when he has acts on the basis of what he considers most probable, and by someone who forgets the prostration before the salutation of peace. The latter must perform two prostrations after his salutation, then perform the testimony *[tashahhud]* and repeat the salutation.

The follower *[ma'mūm]* is not required to perform a prostration for absent-mindedness, unless his prayer leader *[imām]* makes an absent-minded mistake, in which case he must perform prostration together with him. If a leader becomes absent-minded during the prayer, or something happens to affect him badly, it is appropriate for the men in the congregation to exclaim: "Glory be to Allāh! *[Subḥāna 'llāh]*," and for the women to clap their hands.

Chapter

The Ritual Prayer of Voluntary Worship *[Ṣalāt at-Taṭawwu']*

Voluntary ritual prayers are of five types:

1. Those observed as *sunan* [customary practices] and *rawātib* [supererogatory prayers performed before or after the obligatory prayers]. Ibn 'Umar (may Allāh be well pleased with him) described them as follows: "I learned ten cycles from Allāh's Messenger (Allāh bless him and give him peace): two cycles before the midday prayer *[ẓuhr]* and two after it, two cycles after the sunset prayer *[maghrib]* in one's home, two cycles after the evening prayer *['ishā']* in one's home, and two cycles before the dawn prayer *[fajr]*. Ḥafṣa related to me that Allāh's Messenger (Allāh bless him and give him peace) used to perform two cycles when the dawn rose and the muezzin gave the call to prayer, and those two are the most firmly established. It is recommendable to keep them simple, and it is better to perform them at home. The same applies to the two cycles after the sunset prayer."
2. The odd-numbered prayer *[witr]*. Its time is the period between the evening prayer and the dawn prayer. It consists of at least one cycle, and eleven at the most. The closest number to perfection is three, with two salutations of peace. The supplications called *qunūt* should be uttered in the third cycle, while standing after the act of bowing *[rukū']*.
3. Prayers that are absolutely voluntary. Voluntary worship at night is more meritorious than voluntary worship during the daytime, and the last half of the night is better than the first. The night prayer is performed in sets of two cycles. The prayer performed

by someone seated consists of half of the prayer performed by someone standing.

4. Voluntary prayers that are customarily performed in congregation. There are three kinds of these:
   a) The *tarāwīḥ*. They consist of twenty cycles, performed after the evening prayer during Ramaḍān.
   b) The ritual prayer of the eclipse *[ṣalāt al-kusūf]*. When the sun or the moon is eclipsed, the people should seek refuge in the ritual prayer, as a congregation if they wish, and as individuals if they prefer. The worshipper should proceed as follows:

      - Pronounce the affirmation of Allāh's Supreme Greatness.
      - Recite the Opening Sūra of the Qur'ān *[al-Fātiḥa]* and a long Sūra.
      - Perform the act of bowing, and maintain the posture of bowing *[rukūʿ]* for a considerable period of time.
      - Stand upright and recite the Opening Sūra, followed by a long Sūra that is not as long as the previous one.
      - Perform a second act of bowing, less prolonged than the first.
      - Stand upright, then perform two prolonged acts of prostration *[sajdatain]*.
      - Stand upright, then perform the rest of the prayer in similar fashion.

   The complete prayer thus contains four acts of bowing and four acts of prostration.

   c) The ritual prayer for relief from drought *[ṣalāt al-istisqāʾ]*.
   When the earth becomes arid, and there is no sign of rain, the people should go out of town together with the prayer leader. They should set out in their everyday work-clothes, with an attitude of submissiveness, abject humility and earnest entreaty. The prayer leader should lead them in a prayer of two cycles, like the ritual prayer of the Festival *[ṣalāt al-ʿĪd]*. He should then address them with a single sermon, consisting of frequent appeals for forgiveness and the recital of Qurʾānic verses in which pleading for it is commanded. The people should then reverse their outer garments [by moving the part that was on the right shoulder over to the left, and vice-versa].

If the protected non-Muslims *[ahl adh-dhimma]* accompany them, they should not be turned away, but they should be commanded to segregate themselves from the Muslims.

5. Prostration during the recital of the whole Qur'ān *[sujūd at-tilāwa]*. This practice consists of fourteen acts of prostration, two of them performed during recitation of the Sūra of the Pilgrimage *[Sūrat al-Ḥajj]*.[4] The prostration is customarily performed by the reciter and the attentive listener, not by someone who hears the recitation incidentally. The practitioner declares the Supreme Greatness of Allāh when he prostrates himself, and again when he raises his head, then he pronounces the salutation of peace.

[4] When the Sūra of the Pilgrimage is recited, a *sajda* [act of prostration] is performed after the 18th verse, which begins with:

Have you not seen that those in the heavens **make prostration** to Allāh, as do those in the earth, and the sun, the moon, the stars, the hills, the trees, and the beasts, and many of mankind....	*a-lam tara anna 'llāha yasjudu la-hu man fi 's-samāwāti wa man fi 'l-arḍi wa 'sh-shamsu wa 'l-qamaru wa 'n-nujūmu wa 'l-jibālu wa 'sh-shajaru wa 'd-dawābbu wa kathīran mina 'n-nās....*

—and after the 77th, which begins with:

O you who truly believe, bow down and **prostrate yourselves,** and worship your Lord....	*yā ayyuha 'lladhīna āmanu 'rka'ū wa 'sjudū wa ''budū Rabba-kum....*

Chapter

The Times during which the Ritual Prayer is Forbidden

Performance of the ritual prayer is forbidden during these five periods of time:

1. After the dawn prayer *[fajr]* until the rising of the sun.
2. After its rising until it climbs by the measure of a spear.
3. From its momentary halt at the meridian until it declines.
4. After the afternoon prayer *[ʿaṣr]* until the sun wanes close to setting.
5. From when it wanes until it sets.

These are the periods of time during which voluntary prayer may not be performed, with the following exceptions:

- The repetition of the congregational prayer, if it is performed while the worshipper is in the Sacred Mosque.
- The two cycles of prayer performed after completing the circumambulation [around the Kaʿba].
- The funeral prayer.
- Making up for customary supererogatory prayers *[sunan rawātib]* is permissible during two of the [otherwise forbidden] times: namely, after the dawn prayer and after the afternoon prayer.
- Making up for obligatory prayers is also permissible.

Chapter

The Office of the Prayer Leader *[al-Imāma]*

As reported by Abū Mas'ūd al-Badrī (may Allāh be well pleased with him), Allāh's Messenger (Allāh bless him and give him peace) once said:

> The person who leads the people in prayer should be the one among them who is the most competent reciter of the Book of Allāh. If they are equally competent in recitation, he should be the one among them who knows the Sunna best. If they are equal in knowledge of the Sunna, he should be the first among them to have made the *hijra* [migration to Medina]. If they are equal where the *hijra* is concerned, the one who leads them should be the eldest among them. A man should not lead a man in his home, nor in his place of authority, and he should not sit down in his presence, except with his permission.

He also said to Mālik ibn al-Ḥuwairith and his companion, who were almost equally skilled in Qur'ānic recitation:

> When the time of the ritual prayer arrives, let one of you give the call, and let the elder of you act as your leader.

The ritual prayer is not valid when performed behind someone whose prayer is spoiled by impurity, except in the case where the leader is unaware of his own impurity, and the follower is also unaware of it, until he concludes the prayer with the salutation of peace. If the follower then becomes aware of it, he must repeat the prayer on his own. It is also invalid when performed behind someone who omits a basic essential *[rukn]*, except when the local leader prays in a sitting position, because of a sickness that is likely to be cured, in which case the followers should remain seated, unless he begins the prayer while standing, but then becomes weak and sits down, in which case they should stand while praying behind him.

It is not valid for a woman to act as prayer leader for men. As for the person who suffers from incontinence of urine, and the illiterate who does not know the Fātiḥa well, or mispronounces one of its letters, they may not act as prayer leaders except for others like themselves.

It is permissible for someone who has performed the minor ablution *[wuḍūʾ]* to be led by someone who has purified himself with the dry ablution *[tayammum]*, and for someone performing an obligatory prayer to be led by someone whose prayer is supererogatory.

If there is only one follower present, he must station himself to the right of the prayer leader. If he stands to his left, or in front of him, or alone on a spot behind him, his prayer is not valid. If the follower is a woman, however, she must stand alone on a spot behind him. If several followers are present, they should station themselves behind him. It is valid if they stand to his right, or on both sides of him, but not if they stand in front of him or to his left.

When a woman leads women in prayer, she must stand in the middle of their row. The leader of men dressed only in their underclothes must likewise stand in the middle of them. If the congregation consists of men, boys, hermaphrodites and women, the men should be lined up in the first row, the boys in the second, the hermaphrodites in the next, and the women in the last. If someone pronounces the declaration of Allāh's Supreme Greatness before the leader pronounces the salutation of peace, he has arrived in time to join the congregation. If someone arrives in time to perform the act of bowing *[rukūʿ]*, he has caught up with the whole cycle, but otherwise not.

Chapter

The Ritual Prayer of the Sick
[Ṣalāt al-Marīḍ]

If a sick person's illness would be aggravated by his standing up, he should perform the ritual prayer in a sitting position. If he cannot even do that, he should perform it while reclining on his side, because Allāh's Messenger (Allāh bless him and give him peace) once said to ʿImrān ibn Ḥuṣain:

> Perform the prayer while standing, but if you are incapable, then while sitting, and if you are incapable, then on your side.

If reclining on his side is terribly uncomfortable for him, he should lie on his back. If he cannot perform the acts of bowing and prostration, he should signal them by making gestures.

He is obliged to make up for the ritual prayers he has missed during his loss of consciousness. If it is difficult for him to perform each prayer at its prescribed time, he is entitled to combine the midday and afternoon prayers, and the two evening prayers, at the time prescribed for either of the two. If he combines them at the time prescribed for the first, he is obliged to formulate the intention to combine *[niyyat al-jamʿ]* when he performs it, and the excuse must retain its validity until he embarks on the second. He may not separate the two, except by an interval sufficient for the minor ablution *[wuḍūʾ]*. If he postpones [the combined performance], the excuse must retain its validity until the arrival of the time prescribed for the second, and he must have intended the combination at the time prescribed for the first, before becoming unable to perform it.

Combination is permissible for the traveler who is entitled to abbreviate the prayer. It is also permissible to combine the two evening prayers in rainy weather.

Chapter

The Ritual Prayer of the Traveler
[Ṣalāt al-Musāfir]

When the distance of his journey is six parasangs—the distance covered in two days at a steady pace—and provided its purpose is lawful, the traveler is entitled to abbreviate the four-cycle prayers exclusively. This does not apply, however, if he follows a prayer leader who is a local resident, or if he does not formulate the intention to abbreviate, or if he forgets a residential prayer and remembers it on the journey, or a traveling prayer and remembers it when in residence. In all these cases, he is obliged to perform the full-length prayer.

The traveler is allowed to perform the prayer completely, but abbreviation is preferable. If he intends the performance of more than twenty-one prayers, he should perform them completely, but if he does not make that resolution, he should always abbreviate.

Chapter

The Ritual Prayer in Time of Danger *[Ṣalāt al-Khawf]*

The ritual prayer in time of danger *[ṣalāt al-khawf]* is permissible in any manner in which it was performed by Allāh's Messenger (Allāh bless him and give him peace). The preferred version is conducted as follows:

- The prayer leader splits the worshippers into two groups, instructing one group to stand guard, while the other performs one cycle of ritual prayer together with him.
- When he is ready to perform the second cycle, the members of the first group formulate the intention to separate from him, then they complete their prayer and go to stand guard.
- The other group comes and performs the second cycle together with him.
- When he sits for the testimony *[tashahhud]*, the second group stands up and performs another cycle.
- He waits until the second group has pronounced the testimony, then concludes the prayer with the salutation of peace.

If the danger is extremely intense, they should pray while marching and riding, whether facing the *Qibla* or in some other direction, and they should make gestures to indicate the acts of bowing and prostration.

Anyone who is afraid for himself should perform this kind of prayer, in accordance with his situation, and he should do whatever he needs to do in order to escape.

Chapter

The Ritual Prayer of the Friday Congregation *[Ṣalāt al-Jumʿa]*

The Friday congregational prayer is incumbent on every individual for whom the five daily prayers are obligatory—provided that he is a permanent local resident, and the distance between his home and the mosque is no more than a parasang [about four miles].

This rule does not apply to a woman, a slave, a traveler, or someone who is excused because of sickness, or rain, or danger. If they attend the congregation, that is to their credit, but the prayer is not obligatory for them—with the exception of the person whose absence is excusable, for if he is present, he is strictly obliged to perform the prayer.

The validity of the Friday congregational prayer depends on the fulfillment of several preconditions, including the following:

- It must be performed at its prescribed time, in a town or village.
- It must be attended by no fewer than forty of those permanent local residents upon whom it is incumbent.
- It must be preceded by two sermons, and each sermon must include the praising of Allāh (Almighty and Glorious is He), the invocation of blessing on His Messenger (Allāh bless him and give him peace), the recitation of a Qurʾānic verse *[āya]*, and religious exhortation.

It is recommendable for the prayer leader to deliver the sermons from a pulpit. As soon as he has mounted the pulpit, he should turn toward the people and greet them with the salutation of peace. He should then remain seated until the call to prayer has been completed. He should then stand up and deliver the first sermon, then sit down, then deliver the second sermon.

The ritual prayer should then be performed, so he must step down from the pulpit and lead them in two cycles of prayer, reciting the Qur'ānic verses in a clearly audible voice in each cycle.

If someone arrives in time to perform only one cycle with the leader, he should complete the prayer in a Friday congregation, or else at the time of a midday prayer. If the number [of worshippers present] falls short, or the prescribed time expires when they have performed only one cycle, they should likewise complete the prayer in a Friday congregation, or else at the time of a midday prayer.

It is not permissible to perform more than one Friday congregational prayer in the same town or village, unless there is a pressing need for more.

When someone attends the Friday congregational prayer, it is recommendable for him to perform the major ritual ablution, to wear two neat garments, to perfume himself, and to arrive early. If he arrives while the prayer leader is delivering the sermon, he should not sit down until he has performed two cycles of [voluntary] ritual prayer, keeping them short and simple.

It is not permissible for anyone to speak while the prayer leader is delivering the sermon, apart from the leader himself, or someone to whom the leader speaks.

Chapter

The Ritual Prayer of the Two Festivals *[Ṣalāt al-ʿĪdain]*

This is a collective duty *[farḍ ʿala 'l-kifāya]*. Provided that it is performed by forty of the city's inhabitants, the duty is discharged as far as the rest of them are concerned.

The time prescribed for its performance begins when the sun has risen, and ends when the sun has declined from the meridian.

The customary site for its performance is an open space outside the town or village.

In the case of the Festival of Sacrifices *[ʿĪd al-Aḍḥā]*, it is customary to perform the sacrificial slaughter before the prayer, and to break fast afterward. In the case of the Festival of Fastbreaking *[ʿĪd al-Fiṭr]*, on the other hand, the fast is always broken before the prayer is performed.

Those who attend are recommended to perform the major ablution, to wear elegant clothes, and to perfume themselves.

When the time for the prayer arrives, the leader steps forward and leads them in the performance of two cycles, without a call *[adhān]* and without an *iqāmā* [announcement that the prayer is about to begin]. In the first cycle, he utters seven affirmations of Allāh's Supreme Greatness *[takbīrāt]*, as well as the initial *takbīra* of consecration. In the second, he utters five, apart from the *takbīra* pronounced when standing up [after the prostration]. With each *takbīra*, he raises his hands [to the lobes of his ears]. Between every two *takbīra*'s, he praises Allāh and invokes His blessing on the Prophet (Allāh bless him and give him peace). Then he recites the *Fātiḥa* and another Sūra, reciting them both in a clearly audible voice.

After concluding the prayer with the salutation of peace, he delivers two sermons. If it is a Fastbreaking Festival, he should urge the members of the congregation to pay the alms-due, and explain its rules to them. If it is a Festival of Sacrifices, he should explain the rules that apply to sacrificial animals.

The extra *takbīra*'s and the two sermons are a customary practice *[sunna]*.

Supererogatory prayers should not be performed at the site of the Festival prayer, not beforehand and not afterward.

If someone arrives in time to follow the leader before his salutation of peace, he should complete the prayer in the appropriate manner. If someone arrives too late to follow the leader, no making up is required of him, but he may choose to make up for it voluntarily: with an ordinary prayer of two or four cycles, if he wishes, or with a prayer performed in the manner peculiar to the Festival prayer, if he wishes.

It is recommendable to proclaim Allāh's Supreme Greatness during the nights of the Two Festivals, and to proclaim it after the obligatory prayers in congregation during the Festival of Sacrifices, from the dawn prayer on the Day of ʿArafa till the afternoon prayer on the last of the Days of Drying Meat *[Tashrīq]*. The proclamation of Allāh's Supreme Greatness should be uttered twice each time it occurs in the formula:

Allāh is Supremely Great!	*Allāhu Akbar.*
Allāh is Supremely Great!	*Allāhu Akbar.*
There is no god but Allāh!	*Lā ilāha illa 'llāh.*
And Allāh is Supremely Great!	*Wa 'llāhu Akbar.*
Allāh is Supremely Great!	*Allāhu Akbar.*
And to Allāh belongs the praise!	*Wa li'llāhi 'l-ḥamd.*

The Book of the Funeral Rites
[Kitāb al-Janā᾿iz]

The Book of the Funeral Rites
[Kitāb al-Janā'iz]

As soon as it is certain that someone is dead, his eyes should be closed, his jawbones should be locked, and a mirror or something else should be placed on his stomach.

When the ritual washer sets about his task, the dead man's private parts should be screened from view. He should then proceed as follows:

- Squeeze the dead man's stomach with gentle pressure.
- Wrap a piece of cloth around his own hand, and use it to remove the excrement that has been squeezed out.
- Perform the minor ablution *[wuḍū']* on the dead man.
- Wash his head and his beard with water and an extract of lotus.
- Wash the right half of his body, then the left.
- Wash him like that a second time and a third, rubbing his hand over his stomach each time. If anything is excreted from his anus, he should wash it and plug it with cotton. If cotton does not stay in place, he should use pure clay. He should also repeat the minor ablution. If purification is not achieved by three washings, the number should be increased to five or seven.
- Wipe him dry with a towel.

He should then apply perfume to his groins and armpits, and to the parts of the body that touch the ground in *sujūd* [prostration during the ritual prayer]. If he perfumes the whole of his body, that is fine. He should also fumigate his shrouds with perfume. He should trim his mustache and his nails, if they are very long, but he should not comb his hair. If the deceased is a woman, her hair should be braided in three plaits, and they should hang down behind her.

When the purification has been completed, the dead man should be shrouded in three white garments, none of them being a shirt or a turban. The dead woman should be shrouded in five garments: a chemise, a veil, a waist-cloth, and two wrappers.

When the deceased is a man, the following (in order of priority) are the people best entitled to perform his ritual washing, his funeral prayer and his burial: (1) the person to whom he has bequeathed that responsibility; (2) his father; (3) his grandfather; (4) the closest of his paternal male relatives. In the case of a woman, the following are the people best entitled to perform her ritual washing: (1) her mother; (2) her grandmother; (3) the closest of her female relatives. Where the funeral prayer is concerned, however, the governor takes precedence over the father and those next in line.

The leader of the funeral prayer should begin by declaring the Supreme Greatness of Allāh and reciting the Opening Sūra of the Qur'ān *[al-Fātiḥa]*. He should then make a second declaration of Allāh's Supreme Greatness, and invoke blessings upon the Prophet (Allāh bless him and give him peace). Then, after making a third declaration of Allāh's Supreme Greatness, he should say:

O Allāh, forgive our living and our dead, and those of us who are present and those of us who are absent, and our young and our old, and those of us who are male and those of us who are female.	*Allāhumma 'ghfir li-ḥayyi-nā* *wa mayyiti-nā* *wa shāhidi-nā* *wa ghā'ibi-nā* *wa ṣaghīri-nā wa kabīri-nā* *wa dhakari-nā* *wa unthā-nā.*
You surely know our destination and our final resting place, and You are Powerful over all things.	*inna-ka ta'lamu* *munqalaba-nā wa mathwā-nā* *wa Anta 'alā kulli shai'in Qadīr.*
O Allāh, those of us whom You keep alive, let them live in accordance with Islām and the Sunna, and those of us whom You cause to die, let them die in accordance with the same.	*Allāhumma man aḥyaita-hu* *min-nā* *fa-aḥyi-hi 'ala* *'l-Islāmi wa 's-Sunna:* *wa man tawaffaita-hu min-nā* *min-nā fa-tawaffa-hu 'alai-himā.*
O Allāh, forgive him, and have mercy on him, and excuse him, and pardon him.	*Allāhumma 'ghfir la-hu* *wa 'rḥam-hu* *wa 'āfi-hi wa ''fu 'an-hu*

Honor his resting place, and make its entrance wide.	*wa akrim mathwā-hu wa wassi ʿmadkhla-hu*
Wash him with the water of snow and ice,	*wa 'ghsil-hu bi-māʾi 'th-thalji wa 'l-baradi*
and cleanse him of sinful mistakes,	*wa naqqi-hi mina 'l-khaṭāyā*
as white cloth is cleansed of the stain of dirt.	*ka-mā yunaqqa 'th-thawbu 'l-abyaḍu mina 'd-danas.*
Grant him a home that is better than his [earthly] home,	*wa abdil-hu dāran khairan min dāri-hi*
and a spouse who is better than his [earthly] spouse,	*wa zawjan khairan min zawji-hi*
and a family that is better than his [earthly] family.	*wa ahlan khairan min ahl-hi*
Cause him to enter the Garden [of Paradise],	*wa adkhil-hu 'l-jannata*
and protect him from the torment of the tomb	*wa aʿidh-hu min ʿadhābi 'l-qabri*
and from the torment of the Fire [of Hell].	*wa min ʿadhābi 'n-nār.*
Grant him space in his tomb and provide him with light therein.	*wa afsiḥ la-hu fī qabri-hi wa nawwir la-hu fī-h.*

Then, after making a fourth declaration of Allāh's Supreme Greatness, he should turn his face to his right and pronounce a single salutation:

Peace be upon you, and the mercy of Allāh.	*as-salāmu ʿalaikum wa raḥmatu'llāh.*

He should raise his hands with each declaration of Allāh's Supreme Greatness.

The obligatory elements in all that are the declarations of Allāh's Supreme Greatness, the Qurʾānic recitation, the invocation of blessing on the Prophet (Allāh bless him and give him peace), the most appropriate supplication by the living for the deceased, and the salutation of peace.

If someone misses the funeral prayer [at the time of burial], he should perform it over the grave within a month. If the deceased is in a foreign country, he should perform a prayer with the intention of dedicating it to him.

If ritual washing is impracticable for some reason—because of the lack of water, or the risk of decomposition if the corpse is pustulated by smallpox or scorched by fire, or because the deceased is a woman among men, or a man among women—the dry ablution *[tayammum]*[5] should be performed instead. (It is permissible, however, for either of the two spouses to wash the other, and the same applies to the *umm walad* [slave woman who is the mother of her owner's child] and her master.)

If the martyr dies on the battlefield, he should not be washed and the funeral prayer should not be performed over him. He should be stripped of iron and leather armor, then wrapped in his garments of cloth, but if he is shrouded in something else, no harm is done.

If the pilgrim dies while in the state of consecration, he should be washed with water and an extract of lotus. He should not be dressed in stitched cloth, nor be perfumed. His head should not be covered, and neither his hair nor his nails should be clipped.

It is recommendable for the deceased to be buried in a *laḥd* [an oblong excavation in the side of a grave], and for unburned bricks to be stacked on top of the site, as was done at the burial of Allāh's Messenger (Allāh bless him and give him peace). No baked bricks should be inserted into the grave, nor any timber, nor anything touched by fire.

It is recommendable to express condolences to the family of the deceased, and weeping over him is not disapproved, so long as it is not accompanied by wailing or moaning. There is no objection to visiting graves, where men are concerned. When someone passes by them, or visits them, he should say: "Peace be upon you, inhabitants of the abode of believing folk! If Allāh wills, we shall be joining you. O Allāh, do not deprive us of their reward, and do not desert us after them. Forgive us and them. We beg Allāh to grant well-being to us and to you." Whenever someone does a good deed, and assigns its reward to the deceased Muslim, that is to his benefit.

[5] See note 3 on page 19 above.

The Book of the Alms-due
[Kitāb az-Zakāt]

The Book of the Alms-due
[Kitāb az-Zakāt]

The alms-due *[zakāt]* is incumbent on every free Muslim who is in complete possession of a certain minimum *[niṣāb]*. No alms-due is payable on property until it has been in the owner's possession for one whole year, except in the case of the produce of the earth. As for the augmentation of the minimum resulting from *nitāj* [the bringing forth of young animals] and profit, the increase is included in the annual reckoning of the basic property.

The alms-due is payable on four kinds of property only: (1) Grazing livestock. (2) The produce of the earth. (3) Precious metals. (4) Mercantile commodities. No alms-due is payable on any of these, however, until they add up to the minimum. On property that exceeds the minimum, the alms-due is payable on each unit of reckoning, except in the case of grazing livestock, for nothing is payable on their *awqāṣ* [units of which the total is less than the number on which a particular payment is due].

Chapter

The Alms-due on Grazing Livestock *[Zakāt as-Sā'ima]*

The term *sā'ima* signifies grazing livestock, of which there are three kinds:

1. Camels *[ibil]*. On the minimum number, which is five, the alms-due is one *shāt* [sheep or goat]. On ten camels, two sheep or goats are due; on fifteen, three sheep or goats; on twenty, four sheep or goats; on twenty-five, five sheep or goats. On twenty-six to thirty-five, the alms-due is a female camel termed *bint makhāḍ*, which has completed one year of life, or, if none of these is available to him, a male camel termed *ibn labūn*, which has completed two years of life. On thirty-six to forty-five, the alms-due is a female termed *bint labūn*, of the same age as the *ibn labūn*. On forty-six to sixty, it is a female camel termed *ḥiqqa,* which has completed three years of life. On sixty-one to seventy-five, it is a female camel termed *jadha'a makhaḍ,* which means one that has completed its fourth year. On seventy-six to ninety, it is two *bint labūn* she-camels. On ninety-one to one hundred and twenty, it is two *ḥiqqa* she-camels. If the total comes to one more than that, the alms-due is three *bint labūn*. One *ḥiqqa* is then due on every fifty, and one *bint labūn* on every forty. When the total is two hundred, it is divisible by either of these two numbers, so the owner has two options: If he wishes, he may present four *ḥiqqa*, and if he wishes, five *bint labūn*.

   If someone is required to provide a camel of a particular age, but he cannot find one, he has two options: He may present one that is less mature, together with two sheep or goats or twenty silver coins, or, if he wishes, he may present one that is more mature, and receive two sheep or goats or twenty silver coins.

2. Cattle *[baqar]*. On the minimum number, which is thirty, the alms-due is one male *tabīʿ* or female *tabīʿa*, which is the term for a yearling calf. On forty, it is one *musinna*, meaning a female calf that is two years old. On sixty, it is two *tabīʿ* calves. When the number reaches seventy, one *tabīʿ* and one *musinna* are due. Further calculation follows this rule, so that one *tabīʿ* is due on every thirty, and one *musinna* on every forty.
3. Sheep and goats *[ghanam]*. On the minimum number, which is forty, and then up to one hundred and twenty, the alms-due is one sheep or goat. On one hundred and twenty-one to two hundred, it is two sheep or goats; on two hundred and one to three hundred, it is three sheep or goats; for numbers above this, it is one sheep or goat for every hundred.

A billy goat should not be collected in the alms-due, nor a ewe or she-goat that is defective or decrepit, or has recently given birth, or is at the point of giving birth, or is fattened to be eaten. The worst items of the property should not be collected, nor the finest, unless their owners present the latter voluntarily. The only animals to be collected should be females in good health, with the exception of the male calf *[tabīʿ]* that is levied on thirty cattle, and, in the case of camels, the male *ibn labūn* that is substituted for the female *bint makhāḍ*, when the latter is unavailable. This rule does not apply if all the livestock are males or distempered, so one of them will then suffice. In the case of sheep, only the one year old female should be collected, and in the case of goats, only the two year old female. When a camel or calf is collected from the herd, it should be of the age prescribed, unless the owner chooses to present one that is more mature, or they are all immature, so he presents one that is immature. If some of his livestock are in good health and some distempered, some of them are males and some females, and some of them are immature and some mature, he should present a female that is healthy and mature, the value of which is commensurate with the value of the two properties. If his livestock include Bactrian and Arabian camels, cattle and buffaloes, goats and sheep, excellent and inferior specimens, and fat beasts and lean beasts, he should take from each group a selection commensurate with the value of the two properties.

If several people are co-owners of a minimum number of grazing livestock, for one whole year, and they share one pasture, one stallion, one stable, one milking vessel and one drinking trough, their alms-due is governed by the same rule as the alms-due of a single owner. If the prescribed payment is collected from the property of one of them, he is entitled to claim the shares owed by his co-owners. Co-ownership is ineffective except in the case of grazing livestock.

Chapter

The Alms-due on the Produce of the Earth *[Zakāt al-Khārij min al-Arḍ]*

The produce of the earth is of two kinds:

1. Vegetation. The alms-due is payable on all grains and fruits that are measured and stored, when they are produced from the owner's land and amount to five camel-loads, because of the saying of Allāh's Messenger (Allāh bless him and give him peace):

   > There is no alms-due on grains and fruits, until they amount to five camel-loads.

   The camel-load *[wasq]* consists of sixty *ṣā'*, and the *ṣā'* is a *raṭl* according to the Damascus standard [approximately seven pounds], plus an oka *[ūqiyya]* and five-sevenths of an oka. The full amount of the minimum *[niṣāb]* is therefore approximately three hundred and forty-two *raṭl* and six-sevenths of a *raṭl*.

   One tenth is due on produce watered by rain and overflowing rivers, and one twentieth on produce irrigated by artificial means, such as waterwheels and containers transported by camels. As soon as it is obvious that the fruits are healthy and the grains are firm, the alms-due is payable immediately. Grains must not be delivered unless they have been winnowed, nor fruits unless they are dry. There is no alms-due on legitimate earnings consisting of grains and fruits, nor on scattered items picked up from the ground, nor on a wage received for harvesting. No generic type of grain or fruit should be attached to another in the process of completing the minimum *[niṣāb]*. If the minimum consists of a single generic type with different species, like dates, it is subject to the alms-due, and the alms-due should be collected from each species. If someone selects produce of fine quality and excludes that of poor quality, that is permissible and he is entitled to his reward.

2. The contents of a mine. If someone extracts from a mine a minimum quantity of gold or silver, or anything of which the value amounts to a minimum *[niṣāb]*, such as jewels, or antimony, or brass, or iron, it is subject to the alms-due. It must not be delivered until it has been refined and purified.

   Nothing is due on pearls, corals and ambergris, and nothing is due on the hunted game of the land and the sea.

   One fifth is due on buried treasure *[rikāz]* of any kind, whether it be little or much. It is subject to the same tax as booty *[fai']*, and the rest of it belongs to its finder.

Chapter

The Alms-due on Precious Metals *[Zakāt al-Athmān]*

Precious metals are of two kinds: gold and silver. There is no alms-due on silver until its value amounts to two hundred dirhams, at which point five dirhams become due on it. There is no alms-due on gold until its value amounts to twenty dīnārs, at which point half a dīnār become due on it. If either of them contains an adulterating alloy, no alms-due is payable until the quantity of gold and silver amounts to a minimum *[niṣāb]*. If the owner is dubious about that, he has two options: he may deliver the payment, or he may smelt the metals in order to ascertain the fact of the matter.

There is no alms-due on permissible ornaments designed for personal use and lending. Women are permitted to own any gold and silver articles that are customarily worn by them. It is permissible for men to own articles made of silver, such as a signet ring, the adornment of a sword, and the buckle of a belt. As for those that are designed for rental or for storage in a safe, and those that are unlawful to wear, they are subject to the alms-due.

Chapter

The Rule Applied to Debt
[Ḥukm ad-Dain]

If someone has a debt owed to him by an affluent person, or a rightful claim on some property the recovery of which is feasible—like someone whose claim is denied but he has evidence to prove it, or whose property has been usurped but he is capable of regaining it—he is obliged to pay the alms-due on it for the period that has elapsed, as soon as he takes possession of it. On the other hand, if the missing property is irretrievable—like a debt owed by a bankrupt, or a claim that is denied and cannot be proven, and property that has been usurped and gone astray, so there is no hope of finding it—no alms-due is incumbent. The rule applied to the bridal dower is the same as the rule applied to debt.

If someone owes a debt that consumes or diminishes the minimum amount *[niṣāb]* in his possession, no alms-due is incumbent.

Chapter

The Alms-due on Mercantile Commodities *[Zakāt al-ʿUrūḍ]*

There is no alms-due on mercantile commodities until the owner intends to use them for trade, and they constitute a minimum quantity *[niṣāb]* for a full year. He must then appraise their monetary value, and if it comes to no less than a minimum amount of gold and silver, he must pay the alms-due corresponding to their monetary value. If he has some gold or silver in his possession, he must add it to the value of the mercantile commodities when reckoning the *niṣāb*.

So long as the owner intends to use mercantile commodities for private purposes, not for trade, they are not subject to the alms-due. If he later intends to use them for trade, his liability for the alms-due commences on an annual basis.

Chapter

The Alms-due at the Breaking of the Ramaḍān Fast *[Zakāt al-Fiṭr]*

The fast-breaking alms-due *[zakāt al-fiṭr]* is incumbent on every Muslim, provided he has more than the bare necessities of life for himself and his dependents, on the night and the day of the *ʿĪd* [the post-Ramaḍān Festival].

The prescribed amount of this alms-due is one measure of wheat or barley (or the flour or paste of either of these), or of dates or raisins. If someone cannot find any of these, he should provide a measure of any suitable foodstuff that happens to be available to him.

When someone is personally obliged to provide this alms-due, he is also obliged to provide it on behalf of his dependents, on the night of the Festival, if he has the necessary means.

The recommended time for delivering this alms-due is before the ritual prayer on the Day of the Festival. It is not permissible to postpone it beyond the Day of the Festival, but it is permissible to deliver it one or two days earlier. It is permissible to present to one individual the amount prescribed for a group, and vice-versa.

Chapter

The Delivery of the Alms-due
[Ikhrāj az-Zakāt]

It is not permissible for someone to postpone the delivery of the alms-due beyond the time prescribed, if he is capable of delivering it on time. If the article is spoiled as the result of his delay, his liability for the alms-due is not annulled, but it is annulled if the damage occurs in spite of prompt delivery. It is permissible to deliver ahead of the time prescribed, provided the minimum requirement *[niṣāb]* is completely fulfilled.

If someone delivers ahead of the time prescribed, to a person who is not entitled to receive the payment, he has not discharged his obligation, even if that person becomes a qualified recipient at the time when payment is obligatory. On the other hand, if he presents the alms-due to a person who is entitled to receive it, and that person dies, or becomes too rich to qualify, or apostatizes, he has discharged his obligation.

A person may not transport the alms-due to a distant region, so far away that the traveler is allowed to shorten the ritual prayer, unless he cannot find anyone to receive it in his own region.

Chapter

Those to whom the Alms-due may be presented

The alms-due may be presented to eight classes of beneficiaries:

1. The paupers *[fuqarā᾿]*, meaning those who cannot obtain sufficient to meet their needs, either by earning or by other means.
2. The indigent *[masākīn]*, meaning those who have almost everything they need, but are not completely provided for.
3. The agents responsible for collecting the alms-due.
4. Those whose hearts are to be reconciled *[al-mu᾿allafa qulūbu-hum]*. They are the chieftains who command the obedience of their kinsfolk, so the alms-due may be given to them in the hope of dissuading them from doing harm to the Muslims, or of assisting them to collect the alms-due from those who are reluctant to present it.
5. The slaves *[riqāb]*, meaning the *mukātabūn* [slaves who purchase their freedom from their owners].
6. The debtors, meaning those who are under obligation to settle their own debts, or to settle a dispute between two parties among the Muslims.
7. [The volunteers] in the cause of Allāh *[fī sabīli 'llāh]*, meaning those campaigners who are not enlisted in the regular army.
8. The "son of the road" *[ibn as-sabīl]*, meaning the traveler who is far from home, even if he is well-to-do in his home town.

These are the qualified beneficiaries of the alms-due, and it is not permissible to present it to any others. It is permissible to present it to a single individual from among them, because Allāh's Messenger (Allāh bless him and give him peace) commanded the tribe of Zuraiq to present their alms-due to Salama ibn Ṣakhr, and he said to Qubaiṣa:

> Just wait, O Qubaiṣa, until the alms-due comes to us, then we shall order that it should be given to you!

To the pauper and the indigent, one should present enough to satisfy his need; to the agent, enough to cover the expense involved in his agency; to the one to be reconciled, what it takes to effect his reconciliation; to the *mukātab* slave and the debtor, the amount that will settle his debt; to the campaigner, what he needs for his campaign; and to the "son of the road," the cost of his homeward journey. Not one of them should receive more than that. Five of them should not receive anything unless their needs are extremely urgent: namely, the pauper, the indigent, the *mukātab* slave, the debtor who must settle his personal debt, and the "son of the road." It is permissible to present the alms-due to four of them, even when they can manage without it: namely, the agent, the person whose heart is to be reconciled, the campaigner, and the debtor who is under obligation to settle a dispute.

Chapter

Those to whom the Alms-due may not be presented

It is not lawful to present the alms-due to a rich man, nor to a strong man who is capable of earning a livelihood. It is also unlawful to present it to members of the family of Muḥammad (Allāh bless him and give him peace), they being the Banū Hāshim and their clients. It is not permissible to present it to one's parents or grandparents in any generation, nor to one's children or descendants in any generation, nor to a dependent, nor to an unbeliever. As for voluntary almsgiving *[ṣadaqat at-taṭawwuʿ]*, it is permissible for all of the above to be its recipients, as well as other people.

It is not permissible to present the alms-due without a deliberate intention, unless the Imām collects it by force. If someone presents the alms-due to a person who is not entitled to it, he is not fulfilling his obligation, unless the recipient is a rich man whom he supposes to be a pauper.

The Book of the Fast
[Kitāb aṣ-Ṣiyām]

The Book of the Fast
[Kitāb aṣ-Ṣiyām]

The fast of Ramaḍān is obligatory for every Muslim who is an adult, of sound mind, and physically capable of fasting. The minor is also commanded to keep it, if he is able to do so. The beginning of its obligatory observance is marked by one of three things: (1) the completion of the month of Shaʿbān, (2) the sighting of the new moon of Ramaḍān, and (3) the presence of clouds or dust in the air on the night of the thirtieth [of Shaʿbān], obscuring the view of the sky.

If someone sees the new moon when he is by himself, he should begin the fast, and, if he is known to be an honest person, the other people should fast on the strength of his word.

When it comes to breaking the fast at the end of Ramaḍān, the evidence of two honest witnesses is required, and a person may not break it if he is the only one to have sighted the new moon [of Shawwāl].

If people have fasted for thirty days, they should break the fast on the strength of the testimony of two witnesses. They should not break the fast, however, if the sky is cloudy or they have only one person's word, unless they have seen the new moon or completed the maximum number [of days in the month].

If the prisoner of war is dubious about the months, he should make every effort to arrive at a reasonable conclusion, and fast on the basis thereof. Then, if his fast coincides with the month [of Ramaḍān] or one that comes after it, that is sufficient for him [to fulfill his duty], but if it coincides with one that precedes it, that is not sufficient for him [since that year's Ramaḍān still lies ahead].

Chapter

The Rules Applied to Fastbreakers during Ramaḍān

[Aḥkām al-Mufṭirīn fī Ramaḍān]

Breaking fast during Ramaḍān is permissible for these four groups:

1. The sick person who would be harmed by fasting, and the traveler who is entitled to shorten the ritual prayer. Breaking the fast is preferable for them, and they are obliged to make up for it later. If they keep the fast [while sick or while traveling], they are credited with its observance.
2. The woman who is menstruating and the woman in the state of post-natal impurity. They should break the fast and make up for it later. If they keep it, they are not credited with its observance.
3. The pregnant woman and the wet nurse. If they are afraid for themselves, they should break the fast and make up for it later. If they are afraid for their children, they should break the fast and make up for it later, and they must feed a needy person for each day on which the fast is broken.
4. Someone who is incapable of fasting because of old age, or because of a sickness from which he has no hope of recovering. He must compensate by feeding a needy person for each day on which the fast is broken.

For all others who break the fast, there is no obligation apart from making up for it later. The sole exception is someone who breaks the fast by engaging in sexual intercourse, for he must make up for it later and also emancipate a slave. If he cannot find the means to emancipate a slave, he must fast for two months in succession. If he cannot do that, he must feed sixty paupers. If he copulates and does not make expiation until he copulates a second time, a single expiation is required, but if he expiates and then copulates, a second expiation is required. Expiation for engaging in sexual intercourse is incumbent on everyone who is obliged to practice abstinence during Ramaḍān.

If someone postpones making up for a broken fast, with a valid excuse, until another Ramaḍān catches up with him, nothing is required of him apart from making up. If he is guilty of negligence, however, he must feed a needy person for each day, as well as making up. If he refrains from making up until he dies, with a valid excuse, nothing is incumbent upon him. If he does so without a valid excuse, however, he is obliged to compensate by feeding a needy person for each day, unless he has made a solemn vow to fast, in which case it must be fulfilled by fasting. The same rule applies to any solemn vow relating to an act of worshipful obedience.

Chapter

Things that spoil the Fast
[Mā yufsid aṣ-Ṣawm]

If someone does any of the following things, with deliberate intent and while remembering that he is fasting, he spoils the fast:

- Eating, or drinking, or snuffing, or causing a solid or liquid substance to reach into his abdomen from any place whatsoever.
- Masturbating, or kissing, or fondling, or discharging prostatic fluid, or performing a cupping operation, or undergoing a cupping operation.

On the other hand, if he acts while in a state of absent-mindedness, or while subject to coercion, he does not spoil his fast.
His fast is not spoiled in any of the following cases:

- Flies or dust fly into his throat.
- He rinses his mouth or his nose, and some water reaches into his throat.
- He thinks [about sex], and some fluid is sent down or dribbled into his genital gland.
- He experiences an emission of seminal fluid while dreaming.
- Vomiting comes upon him by surprise.

If someone eats when he thinks it is nighttime, but it then becomes clear that it is daytime, he is obliged to make up for breaking the fast. If someone eats when he is dubious about the rising of the dawn, he does not spoil his fast, but if he eats when he is dubious about the setting of the sun, he is obliged to make up for breaking the fast.

Chapter

Voluntary Fasting
[Ṣiyām at-Taṭawwu']

The most meritorious [voluntary] fasting is the fasting of David (peace be upon him), who used to fast and break fast on alternate days. After the month of Ramaḍān, fasting is most meritorious in the month of Allāh called Muḥarram, and of all the days on which righteous work is performed, none are dearer to Allāh than the [first] ten of Dhu'l-Ḥijja. If someone keeps the fast in Ramaḍān, and follows it with six days of Shawwāl, it is as if he had fasted throughout the entire year. Fasting on the Day of 'Āshūrā' is the atonement for the sins of a year, and fasting on the Day of 'Arafa is the atonement for the sins of two years. For someone who is present at 'Arafa, however, keeping the fast is not recommended. Fasting is recommended on the days of the white nights [the thirteenth, fourteenth and fifteenth of the month], and on the second and the fifth.

The practitioner of voluntary fasting is his own commander. If he wishes, he may fast, and if he wishes, he may break fast, without being obliged to make up for it. The same rule applies to all other voluntary religious practices, except the Pilgrimage and the Visitation *['Umra]*, for they must be performed completely, and it is necessary to make up for anything in them that is spoiled.

Allāh's Messenger (Allāh bless him and give him peace) prohibited fasting on two days: namely, the Day of Breaking Fast [at the end of Ramaḍān] and the Day of the Sacrificial Offerings [at the end of the Pilgrimage]. He also prohibited fasting on the Days of *Tashrīq* [the three days immediately following the Day of the Sacrificial Offerings], although he did allow it in the case of the *mutamatti'* [someone who takes advantage *(yatamatta')* of his presence in Mecca on a Visitation by performing the Pilgrimage in the same year], if he cannot afford to make a sacrificial offering. He also allowed it during the Night of Power, which is one of the last ten nights of Ramaḍān.

Chapter

Worshipful Seclusion
[al-Iʿtikāf]

The term *iʿtikāf* signifies seclusion in the mosque for the purpose of worshipful obedience to Allāh (Exalted is He). It is a meritorious customary practice *[sunna]*, unless it is undertaken as solemn vow, in which case its fulfillment obligatory.

Its observance by a woman is valid in any place of worship, apart from the place of worship in her home. Its observance by a man is not valid, however, except in a mosque in which the congregational prayer is performed, and his worshipful seclusion is best observed in a mosque where the Friday prayer *[jumʿa]* is performed.

If someone vows to practice worshipful seclusion or the ritual prayer in a particular mosque, he is entitled to do that in any other, except in the case of the three mosques [in Mecca, Medina and Jerusalem]. If he vows to practice it in the Sacred Mosque [in Mecca], he is obliged to do so. If he vows to practice worshipful seclusion in the Mosque of Allāh's Messenger (Allāh bless him and give him peace) [in Medina], it is permissible for him to practice it in the Sacred Mosque. If he vows to practice worshipful seclusion in the Mosque of al-Aqṣā [in Jerusalem], he is entitled to do so in whichever of the two he prefers [either the Mosque of al-Aqṣā or the Sacred Mosque].

The practitioner of worshipful seclusion is recommended to keep himself occupied with some activity that will bring him close to Allāh (Exalted is He), and to abstain from things that do not concern him, in word and in deed, so as not to nullify the worshipful seclusion. He must not go outside of the mosque, except for some unavoidable reason, unless his temporary departure has been stipulated as a precondition, and he must not consort with a woman. If he inquires about a sick person on his way, or about someone else, but does not turn aside to visit him, that is permissible.

The Book of the Pilgrimage and the Visitation

[Kitāb al-Ḥajj wa 'l-ʿUmra]

The Book of the Pilgrimage and the Visitation *[Kitāb al-Ḥajj wa 'l-ʿUmra]*

Performance of the Pilgrimage *[Ḥajj]* and the Visitation *[ʿUmra]* is an obligatory duty, once in a lifetime, for every Muslim who is an adult, of sound mind, and free [from slavery], provided that he can find the necessary means.

He must be capable of acquiring provisions for the journey, a riding camel, and the kind of equipment suitable for a person like himself, in addition to what he needs to settle his debts, and to support himself and his dependents on a permanent basis.

A woman should be accompanied by a man who is her *maḥram*, that is to say, her husband or someone to whom she could never be lawfully married, because of consanguinuity or for some other legally valid reason.

If someone neglects his duty until he dies, the cost of a Pilgrimage and a Visitation should be collected from his estate.

The Pilgrimage is not valid when performed by an unbeliever or a lunatic. It is valid when performed by a minor and a slave, though it is not obligatory for either of them. It is also valid when performed by someone who lacks the proper means, and by a woman who is not accompanied by a *maḥram*.

If someone performs the Pilgrimage on behalf of another person, when he has not performed it on his own behalf, or to fulfill his vow, or as a supererogatory observance, or if he performed it before the Pilgrimage of Islām was established, his Pilgrimage fulfills his own obligatory duty, not that of another person.

Chapter

The Starting Points
[al-Mawāqīt]

The starting points [where travelers enter the state of consecration before proceeding to perform the Pilgrimage] are the following:

For the people of Medina: **Dhu'l-Ḥulaifa**
For the people of Syria, the West and Egypt: **al-Juḥfa**
For the people of Yemen: **Yalamlam**
For the people of Najd: **Qarn [al-Manāzil]**
For the people of the East: **Dhāt ʿIrq**

These starting points are for their local inhabitants, and also for everyone who passes by them. If someone's place of residence is nearer [to Mecca] than the starting point, his state of consecration begins at home. The people of Mecca enter the state of consecration from the city itself, in preparation for their Pilgrimage, and from the nearest place outside the sacred territory, in preparation for the Visitation. If someone's road does not lead to an starting point, he should enter the state of consecration at a place adjacent to the one that is closest to him.

For someone who intends to enter Mecca, it is not permissible to pass by the starting point without being in the state of consecration, except to wage a lawful battle, or to meet a frequently recurring need, such as the gathering of firewood. Then, if he intends to perform the rites, he should enter the state of consecration from his place. If he passes beyond it without being in the state of consecration, he should go back and enter the state of consecration from the starting point. No expiatory sacrifice of animal blood will then be incumbent on him, because he has entered the state of consecration from his starting point. On the other hand, if he enters the state of consecration from a point closer to Mecca, an expiatory sacrifice of animal blood is incumbent on him, whether or not he returns to the starting point.

It is better for the pilgrim traveler to refrain from entering the state of consecration before he reaches the starting point, but if he does, he is consecrated.

The months of the Pilgrimage are Shawwāl, Dhu'l-Qaʿda, and ten days of Dhu'l-Ḥijja.[6]

[6] This is the traditional interpretation of:

[The time of] the Pilgrimage is certain well-known months. (Q. 2:197)	*al-Ḥajju ashhurun maʿlūmun.*

Chapter

The State of Consecration *[al-Iḥrām]*

When someone intends to enter the state of consecration *[iḥrām]*, it is recommendable for him to proceed as follows:

He should perform the major ablution, make himself neat and tidy, and freshen himself with perfume.

Having divested himself of all tailored clothing, he should wear an *izār* [seamless waist-wrapper] and a *ridā'* [seamless piece of cloth over his shoulder], both of them white and clean.

He should then perform two cycles of ritual prayer, with the intention of entering the state of consecration. It is also recommendable for him to state the particular purpose for which he has consecrated himself, and to stipulate a precondition, by saying:

O Allāh, I intend to perform the rites of such-and-such,	*Allāhumma innī urīdu 'n-nusuka 'l-fulānī:*
so if anything detains me, my place will be wherever You detain me.	*fa-in ḥabasa-nī ḥābisun fa-maḥallī ḥaithu ḥabasta-nī.*

He has the following three options, in order of preference: (1) He may choose *tamattu'*, which means that he consecrates himself for the Visitation *['Umra]* during the months of the Pilgrimage, then, having performed it, he consecrates himself for the Pilgrimage *[Ḥajj]* in the same year. (2) He may choose *ifrād* [separation], which means that he consecrates himself for the Pilgrimage alone. (3) He may choose *qirān* [combination], which means that he consecrates himself for both of them, or that he consecrates himself for the Visitation and then includes the Pilgrimage. If he consecrates himself for the Pilgrimage and then includes the Visitation, his consecration for the Visitation is not effective.

As soon as he is firmly seated on his riding camel, he must say:

Doubly at Your service, O Allāh!	*labbai-ka Allāhumma*
Doubly at Your service!	*labbai-k:*
No partner have You!	*lā sharīka la-ka*
Doubly at Your service!	*labbai-k:*
Yours is the praise and the gracious favor,	*inna 'l-ḥamda wa 'n-ni'mata la-ka*
and Yours is the kingdom!	*wa 'l-mulku la-k:*
No partner have You!	*lā sharīka la-k.*

It is recommendable to repeat this [declaration called the *talbiyya*] many times, and to do so in a loud voice, except in the case of women. It is imperative on the following occasions:

- When climbing an elevated place or going down into a valley.
- On hearing another person uttering the *talbiyya*.
- After the negligent commission of some forbidden act.
- When meeting up with a caravan.
- Immediately after each of the five daily prayers.
- In the time before dawn, and at the onset of the night and of the day.

Chapter

Things Forbidden in the State of Consecration *[Maḥẓūrāt al-Iḥrām]*

There are nine of these:

1,2. Shaving the hair and clipping the nails. Three infractions incur a *dam* [sacrificial offering of animal blood]. For any lesser number, expiation is made by offering food amounting to one quarter of a cubic measure *[ṣāʿ]*. If hair gets into someone's eye, so he plucks it out, or his hair hangs down and covers his eyes, or his nail breaks, so he clips it, no expiation is required of him.

3. Wearing stitched clothes, except when a person cannot find a seamless waist-wrapper, so he wears trousers, or he cannot find a pair of sandals, so he wears a pair of shoes, in which case no expiatory sacrifice is required of him.
4. Covering the head. The ears are counted as part of the head.
5. The application of perfume to the body and clothes.
6. The killing of game, meaning any wild animal that may be hunted for food [at other times]. As for domestic animals, it is not unlawful to kill them. As for the game of the sea, it is permissible.
7. Contracting marriage is unlawful, but no expiatory sacrifice is incurred thereby.
8. Sexual contact short of the vulva. If he ejaculates sperm because of it, he is obliged to sacrifice a *badana* [she-camel or cow]. If not, he must sacrifice a sheep or goat. His Pilgrimage is then valid.
9. Copulation in the vulva. If this occurs before the first lawful deconsecration *[taḥallul]*, the Pilgrimage is annulled. The offender must complete its rites, despite its annulment, and perform the

Pilgrimage in a later year. He must also sacrifice a she-camel or cow. If the offense is committed after the first lawful deconsecration, he must sacrifice a sheep or goat. He must also abstain from self-indulgence, in order to perform the circumambulation in a state of consecration. If he copulates during the Visitation, he renders it null and void. The rites [of Pilgrimage and Visitation] are not annulled by any other offense.

The same rules apply to the woman as to the man, except that her consecration includes veiling her face, and she is entitled to wear stitched clothing.

Chapter

The Expiation
[al-Fidya]

This falls into two categories:

1. The type in which the offender is free to choose any of several options. If someone violates the rules that apply to the hair and nails, to clothing and to perfume, he has three choices: (1) Fasting for three days. (2) Feeding six needy people with three measures of dates. (3) Slaughtering a sheep or goat. If someone kills game, his expiation consists of the equivalent of what he has killed, in the case of animals. In the case of birds, he must provide their monetary value, with the exception of the dove, for which a sheep or goat must be sacrificed, and the ostrich, for which the required expiation is a she-camel or cow. As an alternative to sacrificing the equivalent, he may choose to provide one measure of food for each needy person, or to substitute one day of fasting for each measure of food.
2. The type in which the options are arranged in order of priority. In the case of the *mutamatti'* [someone who consecrates himself for the Visitation *['Umra]* during the months of the Pilgrimage, then, having performed it, consecrates himself for the Pilgrimage *[Ḥajj]* in the same year], he is obliged to expiate by sacrificing a sheep or goat. If that is beyond his means, he is obliged to fast for three days during the Pilgrimage, and for seven days when he has returned to his home.

In the case of sexual intercourse, the expiation is a she-camel or cow. If that is beyond the offender's means, he is obliged to fast in the same manner as the *mutammati'*.

The same rule applies to the *dam* [sacrificial offering of animal blood] which is required to rectify the omission of an essential element of the Pilgrimage. If someone is prevented from returning to his home, he is obliged to make a sacrificial offering of animal blood, but if that is beyond his means, he must fast for ten consecutive days.

If someone repeats a forbidden act of the same kind, other than the killing of game, a single atonement is required, unless he atones for the first before committing the second. If he commits several forbidden acts of different kinds, an atonement is required for each one.

In certain cases, expiation is required regardless of whether the offense was committed with deliberate intent or absent-mindedly: namely, shaving the hair and clipping the nails, sexual intercourse, and the killing of game. No expiation is required for the absent-minded commission of the other forbidden acts.

Every sacrificial offering and provision of food must be presented to the needy folk within the Meccan Sanctuary, apart from the expiation of shaving, which must be distributed in the place where the offender shaves his hair, and the sacrificial offering of the offender whose movement is restricted, for he must slaughter it in his place. As for fasting, it may be observed in any location.

Chapter

Entering Mecca [Dukhūl Makka]

The pilgrim is recommended to enter Mecca from its highest side, and to enter the Sacred Mosque through the Banī Shaiba Gate, because the Prophet (Allāh bless him and give him peace) entered through it.

When he sees the House *[al-Bait]*, he should raise his hands as he proclaims the Supreme Greatness of Allāh, praises Him, and utters a prayer of supplication.

He should then begin the circumambulation of the Visitation *[ʿUmra]*, if he is a visitant *[muʿtamir]*, or the circumambulation of arrival, if he is a *mufrid* [one who has consecrated himself for the Pilgrimage alone] or a *qārin* [one who has consecrated himself for both the Pilgrimage and the Visitation]. He should wear his *ridāʾ* [the wrapper for the upper part of his body] in such a way that its centerpiece is tucked under his right armpit, and its two edges are draped over his left shoulder. At the start of his circumambulation [around the Kaʿba], he should approach the Black Stone *[al-Ḥajar al-Aswad]*, touch it with his hand, kiss it, and say:

In the Name of Allāh,	*Bismi'llāhi*
and Allāh is Supremely Great!	*wa 'llāhu Akbar.*
O Allāh! With faith in You	*Allāhumma īmānan bi-ka*
and belief in Your Book,	*wa taṣdīqan bi-ka*
and in fulfillment of	*wa bi-Kitābi-ka*
Your covenant,	*wa wafā'an bi-ʿahdi-ka*
and following the example	*wa 'ttibāʿan li-sunnati*
of Your Prophet Muḥammad	*Nabiyyi-ka Muḥammad*
(Allāh bless him and give him peace!)	*(ṣalla 'llāhu ʿalaihi wa sallam).*

He should then move to his right, with the House on his left, and circumambulate seven times, moving at a very brisk pace during the first three circuits from the Stone to the Stone. He should walk at a leisurely pace during the last four circuits, and whenever he reaches the Yamānī Corner and the Black Stone, he should touch them with his hand, while exclaiming:

Allāh is Supremely Great!	*Allāhu Akbar.*
There is no god but Allāh!	*Lā ilāha illa 'llāh*

Between the two corners, he should say:

Our Lord! Grant us good in this world and good in the Hereafter, and save us from the torment of the Fire!	*Rabbanā ātinā fi 'd-dunyā ḥasanatan wa fi'ākhirati ḥasana: wa qinā ʿadhāba 'n-nār.*

To this he may add any other supplications that he wishes to make.

When he has completed his circumambulation, he should perform two cycles of ritual prayer behind the Station of Abraham *[Maqām Ibrāhīm]*, then return to the Corner and touch it.

Next, he should go out [of the Sacred Mosque] to [the small hill of] aṣ-Ṣafā, by way of the gate of that name. Having climbed the hill, he should say:

Allāh is Supremely Great!	*Allāhu Akbar.*
There is no god but Allāh!	*Lā ilāha illa 'llāh.*

—and offer a supplication to Allāh.

He should then go down [the hill of aṣ-Ṣafā] and walk at a leisurely pace to the first mile-post. Then he should move at a rapid pace until he reaches the last mile-post. From this point he should slacken his pace until he reaches [the small hill of] al-Marwa, where he should repeat what he did on aṣ-Ṣafā.

He should then descend [from al-Marwa], walking at an easy pace over the appropriate stretch, and almost running where a brisk pace *[saʿy]* is called for, until he arrives at aṣ-Ṣafā. He must then repeat the whole procedure, until he has covered seven laps, starting out from aṣ-Ṣafā and ending up at al-Marwa.

Once he has finished doing all this, he may cut his hair short, if he is a *mutamattiʿ* [someone who consecrates himself for the Visitation *[ʿUmra]* during the months of the Pilgrimage, then, having performed

it, consecrates himself for the Pilgrimage *[Ḥajj]* in the same year], for he is no longer in the state of consecration. This does not apply to the *mutamatti‘* if he has brought a sacrificial animal with him, nor to the *qārin* [one who has consecrated himself for both the Pilgrimage and the Visitation] and the *mufrid* [one who has consecrated himself for the Pilgrimage alone], for they are still in the state of consecration.
The woman follows the same procedures as the man, except that she does not move briskly during the circumambulation, and she does not move at a rapid pace [between aṣ-Ṣafā and al-Marwa].

Chapter

Description of the Pilgrimage
[Ṣifat al-Ḥajj]

On the Day of *Tarwiyya*,[7] someone who is not in the state of consecration must enter that state in Mecca, and go out to ʿArafāt.

When the sun has declined from the meridian on the Day of ʿArafa, he must perform the midday and afternoon prayers, combining the two with a single call *[adhān]* and two *iqāma*'s [announcements that the prayer is about to begin]. He must then proceed to the Standing-place *[mawqif]*—and the whole of ʿArafāt is a Standing-place, with the exception of the gully called Baṭn ʿIrna. It is recommendable for him to stand at the Standing-place of the Prophet (Allāh bless him and give him peace), or close to it on the Mount of Mercy, near to the rocks. He should hold the pedestrians' rope between his hands, and turn toward the *Qibla*, as he moves up like a rider. He should frequently exclaim:

There is no god but Allāh Alone.	*Lā ilāha illa 'llāhu Waḥda-h:*
No partner has He.	*lā sharīka la-h.*
To Him belongs the kingdom	*la-hu 'l-mulku*
and to Him belongs the praise.	*wa la-hu 'l-ḥamd.*
He brings to life and causes death,	*yuḥyī wa yumītu*
while He is Ever-Living and never dies.	*wa huwa Ḥayyun lā yamūt*
All goodness is in His Hand,	*bi-yadi-hi 'l-khairu*
and He is Powerful over all things.	*wa Huwa ʿalā kulli shaiʾin Qadīr.*

[7] In this context, the word *tarwiyya* has two possible meanings: (1) Providing water; (2) Deliberation, reflection, pondering. According to some Islamic authorities, the eighth of Dhu'l-Ḥijja is the day on which the pilgrims provide themselves with water for the visit to Minā. According to others, however, it is called the Day of *Tarwiyya* to commemorate the fact that this was the day on which Abraham (peace be upon him) pondered over the sacrifice he had been commanded to make of his son.

He may use his own judgment in formulating supplications and appeals to Allāh (Almighty and Glorious is He), until the setting of the sun.

He should then set out for Muzdalifa along the road between two mountains, in company with the Imām. He should maintain a calm and dignified bearing, while declaring his readiness to serve and remembering Allāh (Almighty and Glorious is He).

Once he has reached Muzdalifa, he should perform the sunset and evening prayers, combining the two, then set up camp and spend the night there.

Then, after performing the dawn prayer in the darkness of the last part of the night, he should make his way to the Sacred Monument *[al-Maʿshar al-Ḥarām]*,[8] stand beside it and offer a supplication. His supplication should preferably be expressed in the following words:

O Allāh, as You have	*Allāhumma ka-mā*
caused us to stand here,	*awqafta-nā fī-h:*
and have let us see it	*wa araita-nā iyyā-h:*
[this Sacred Monument],	
help us to practice	*fa-waffiq-nā*
remembrance of You,	*li-dhikri-ka*
according to the guidance	*ka-mā hadaita-nā*
You have given us.	
And forgive us	*wa 'ghfir la-nā*
and have mercy on us,	*wa 'rḥam-nā*
as You have promised us	*ka-mā waʿadta-nā*
in Your own words	*bi-qawli-ka*
(and Your words are the Truth!):	*(wa qawlu-ka 'l-Ḥaqq):*
"And when you press on in the	*fa-idhā afaḍtum min ʿArafātin*
multitude from ʿArafāt,	
remember Allāh by the	*fa-'dhkuru 'llāha ʿinda'*
Sacred Monument.	*l-Mashʿari 'l-Ḥarām:*
Remember Him as He has	*wa'dhkurū-hu ka-mā*
guided you aright, even though,	*hadā-kum wa in kuntum*
before this, you were among	*min qabli-hi*
those who have gone astray.	*la-mina 'ḍ-ḍāllīn:*

[8] The Sacred Monument *[al-Maʿshar al-Ḥarām]* marks the spot in Muzdalifa (about midway between ʿArafāt and Minā) where the Prophet (Allāh bless him and give him peace) offered up a long prayer of supplication.

Then pass on quickly from the place from which the multitude is quick to pass on,	*thumma afīḍū min* *ḥaithu afāḍa 'n-nāsu*
and ask forgiveness of Allāh. Allāh is indeed Forgiving, Merciful. (Q. 2:198,199)	*wa 'staghfiru 'llāh:* *inna 'llāha Ghafūrun Raḥīm.*

He should stand there until the light of day is glowing brightly, then move on before the rising of the sun. When he reaches the Valley of Maḥsir, he should run at top speed until he comes to Minā, then perform the rite of stoning the three Satanic pillars. Beginning with the pillar called *jamrat al-ʿAqaba*, he should pelt each one with seven pebbles, like the pebbles shot from a catapult. He should raise both hands while throwing, and accompany each pebble with the proclamation of Allāh's Supreme Greatness. He should discontinue the *talbiyya* at the beginning of the rite of stoning.

Then, having gone down into the valley, he should turn toward the *Qibla*, but he should not stand there. He should then slaughter his sacrificial offering. He may also shave his head or cut his hair short, for everything [forbidden in the state of consecration] is now lawful to him, apart from women.

He should then press on to Mecca with the crowd, and there perform the rite called *ṭawāf az-ziyāra*, which is the obligatory circumambulation that marks the completion of the Pilgrimage.

At this point, if he is a *mutamattiʿ*, or one of those who have not performed the rite of *saʿy* after the circumambulation on first arrival [*ṭawāf al-qudūm*], he should run to and fro between aṣ-Ṣafā and al-Marwa, Everything [forbidden while in the state of consecration] will then become lawful to him again.

For anyone who wishes to do so, it is recommendable to drink water from the well of Zamzam, and to sprinkle himself with it, then say:

O Allāh, let it be for us a [source of] useful knowledge, and ample sustenance, and a quenching and a satisfaction, and a remedy for every sickness. And wash with it my heart, then fill it with Your awesomeness and Your wisdom!	*Allāhumma 'jʿal-hu la-nā* *ʿilman nāfiʿan* *wa rizqan wāsiʿa wa rayyan* *wa shabʿan wa shabʿan* *wa shifāʾan min kulli dāʾ:* *wa 'ghsil bi-hi qalbī* *wa 'mlaʾ-hu min khashyati-ka* *wa ḥikmati-k.*

Chapter

What is Done after Deconsecration *[al-Ḥill]*

The pilgrim should then return to Minā and spend three nights there. During the daytime, after the sun's decline from the meridian, he should perform the rite of stoning the Satanic pillars, casting seven pebbles at each pillar. Starting with the first pillar *[al-jamrat al-ūlā]*, he should throw seven pebbles at it, while facing the *Qibla*—as he threw them earlier at the pillar called *jamrat al-ʿAqaba*—then stand and offer a supplication to Allāh. He should then approach the middle pillar *[al-jamrat al-wusṭā]*, and stone it in the same manner. Then he should stone the pillar called *jamrat al-ʿAqaba*, but he should not stand beside it [after casting the pebbles]. He should repeat the rite of stoning on the second day, in precisely the same manner. If he prefers to stay no longer than two days, he must leave before sunset. If the sun sets while he is still at Minā, he is obliged to spend the night there, and to perform the rite of stoning on the following day.

If he is a *mutamattiʿ*, or a *qārin* [one who has consecrated himself for both the Pilgrimage and the Visitation], his Pilgrimage and his Visitation are now concluded.

If he is a *mufrid* [one who has consecrated himself for the Pilgrimage alone], he has now passed into the state of deconsecration, so he must consecrate himself for the Visitation. On leaving Minā, he should go to Mecca, perform the rites of circumambulation [around the Kaʿba] and *saʿy* [running to and fro between aṣ-Ṣafā and al-Marwa], and then shave his head or cut his hair short. If he has no hair, it is recommendable for him to pass the razor over his head. His Pilgrimage and his Visitation are now completed.

The responsibility of the *qārin* does not exceed that of the *mufrid*, but the *qārin* and the *mutamatti*ʿ are required to provide a sacrificial offering of animal blood, because Allāh (Exalted is He) has said:

If someone performs the Visitation and stays on for the Pilgrimage,	*fa-man tamattaʿa bi'l-ʿUmrati ila 'l-Ḥajji*
he must make the kind of offering that he can easily afford.	*fa-ma 'staisara mina 'l-hady:*
But if someone cannot afford it, a fast of three days during the Pilgrimage, and of seven when you have returned. (2:196)	*fa-man lam yajid fa-ṣiyāmu thalāthati ayyāmin fi 'l-Ḥajji wa sabʿatin idhā rajaʿtum.*

When someone intends to set out for home, he should not depart until he has taken leave of the House [of Allāh] with a farewell circumambulation, once he has completed all his business affairs, so that his final commitment will be to the House. If he engages in trade after that, he should repeat the farewell circumambulation. In the course of his circumambulation, it is recommendable for him to halt at the *multazam* [the space in the wall which pilgrims hug to their breasts], between the corner and the door, and cling to the House while saying:

O Allāh, this is Your House, and I am Your servant, the son of Your servant and the son of your maidservant!	*Allāhumma hādha Baitu-ka wa ana ʿabdu-ka wa 'bnu ʿabdi-ka wa 'bnu amati-ka*
You have transported me on those of Your creatures which You have made subservient to me,	*ḥamalta-nī ʿalā mā sakhkharta lī min khalqi-ka*
and You have caused me to travel through Your lands,	*wa sayyarta-nī fī bilādi-ka*
until You brought me to my destination by Your gracious favor.	*ḥattā ballaghta-nī bi-niʿmati-k.*
You have also helped me to perform my pilgrim rites,	*wa aʿanta-nī ʿalā qaḍā'i nusukī*
so if You are well pleased with me, may You approve of me even more!	*fa-in kunta raḍīta ʿan-nī fa-'zdid ʿan-nī riḍā*

Or at least bestow Your grace upon me now,	*wa illā fa-manni ʿalayya 'l-āna*
before my departure from Your House!	*qabla tabāʿudī ʿan Baiti-k:*
This is the moment of my leaving, if You will permit me,	*hādha awānu 'nṣirāfī in adhinta lī*
as one who seeks no substitute	*ghairi mustabdilin bi-ka*
for You nor for Your House,	*wa lā bi-Baiti-ka*
and who is not eager to leave	*wa lā rāghibin ʿan-ka*
You nor to leave Your House.	*wa lā ʿan Baiti-k:*
O Allāh! So let me be	*Allāhumma fa-aṣḥib-ni*
accompanied by fitness in my frame,	*'l-ʿāfiyata fī badanī*
and good health in	*wa 'ṣ-ṣiḥḥata fī jismī*
my body, and virtuousness in my religion!	*wa 'l-ʿiṣmata fī dīnī*
And let my ultimate outcome be a good one,	*wa aḥsin munqalabī*
and bless me with obedience	*wa 'rzuq-nī ṭāʿata-ka*
to You, as long as You keep me alive,	*mā abqaita-nī*
and grant me the good	*wa 'jmaʿ lī khaira*
things of both this world	*'d-dunyā*
and the Hereafter!	*wa 'l-ākhirati*
Surely You are Powerful over all things!	*inna-ka ʿalā kulli shaiʾin Qadīr.*

He should add any other supplication he may wish to offer, then invoke blessing on the Prophet (Allāh bless him and give him peace).

If someone departs before the farewell circumambulation, he should come back and perform it, if he is still close by. If he is too far away, he should send a sacrificial offering.

No farewell circumambulation is required of a woman who is menstruating, nor of one who is in the post-natal state of impurity, but it is recommendable for them to stand at the door of the Mosque and offer suplication.

Chapter

The Basic Essentials of the Pilgrimage and the Visitation *[Arkān al-Ḥajj wa 'l-ʿUmra]*

The basic essentials *[arkān]* of the Pilgrimage are:

1. The rite of standing at ʿArafa *[al-wuqūf bi-ʿArafa]*.
2. The circumambulation of the visit *[ṭawāf az-ziyāra]*.

Its necessary elements *[wājibāt]* are:

1. Entering the state of consecration *[iḥrām]* at the starting point *[mīqāt]*.
2. Standing at ʿArafa until nightfall.
3. The overnight stop at Muzdalifa, until after midnight.
4. The rite of *saʿy* [running to and fro between aṣ-Ṣafā and al-Marwa].
5. The overnight stay at Minā.
6. The casting of pebbles *[ramy]* at the Satanic pillars.
7. Shaving the head.
8. The farewell circumambulation *[ṭawāf al-wadāʿ]*.

As for the Visitation *[ʿUmra]*, its essential element is the state of consecration *[iḥrām]*.

Its necessary elements *[wājibāt]* are:

1. The state of consecration *[iḥrām]*.
2. The rite of *saʿy* running to and fro between aṣ-Ṣafā and al-Marwa.
3. Shaving the head.

If someone omits a basic essential, he cannot complete his rites without it. If someone omits a necessary element, he should rectify the omission by making a sacrifice of animal blood. If someone omits a customary observance *[sunna]*, he incurs no liability.

If someone does not stand at ʿArafa until the dawn appears on the Day of Immolation *[Yawm an-Naḥr]*, he has missed the Pilgrimage. He should deconsecrate himself by performing a circumambulation and a *saʿy*, and immolate a sacrificial animal, if he has one with him. It is incumbent upon him to make up for the missed Pilgrimage.

If all the people are mistaken about the date, so they perform the rite of standing on a day other than the Day of ʿArafa, that is sufficient for them. If a group of them do that, however, they have missed the Pilgrimage.

It is recommendable for someone who performs the Pilgrimage to visit the tomb of the Prophet (Allāh bless him and give him peace) and the tombs of his two Companions [Abū Bakr and ʿUmār] (may Allāh be well pleased with them both).

Chapter

The Sacrificial Offerings called *al-Hady and al-Uḍḥiyya* [9]

These sacrificial offerings are a customary practice *[sunna]*, which is not obligatory except in fulfillment of a solemn vow. The offering of a sacrificial animal is more meritorious than giving its price as a charitable donation.

The animals most suitable for sacrifice are camels, then bovines, and then sheep or goats. It is recommendable to make sure that they are in excellent condition, bearing plenty of flesh and fat.

In the case of sheep, only the *jadhaʿ* is acceptable, while the *thanī* is acceptable in other cases. As for the *jadhaʿ*, it is an animal that is fully six months old, while the term *thanī* is applied to a goat that is one year old, to a bovine that is two years old, and to a camel that is five years old.

A sheep or goat is acceptable as a sacrificial offering from a single individual, and a fat camel or bovine as a collective offering from a group of seven.

The following specimens are unsuitable [because of their serious defects]:

- A one-eyed creature *[ʿawrāʾ]* whose one-eyed condition is clearly apparent.
- An emaciated animal *[ʿajfāʾ]* that is unclean.
- A lame animal *[ʿarjāʾ]* whose limping is clearly apparent.
- An animal so sick *[marīḍa]* that its sickness is clearly apparent.
- An animal that has a broken horn or a slit ear *[ʿaḍbāʾ]*, meaning one that has lost the greater part of one of its ears or horns.

[9] The *hady* is a sacrificial offering presented for the purpose of expiation. The *uḍḥiyya* is sacrificed in the rite of Pilgrimage called *ʿId al-Aḍḥā* [the Festival of Sacrifices].

The following are suitable [because their defects are considered less serious]:

- A completely hornless ewe *[jammāʾ]*.
- An animal whose tail has been cut off *[batrāʾ]*.
- A gelding *[khaṣī]*.
- An animal with an ear of which less than half has been split, pierced, or cut off.

In accordance with the customary practice *[sunna]*, a camel should be immolated in a standing posture, with its left foot hobbled, while bovines and sheep and goats should be slaughtered on their sides. The slaughterer should say:

In the Name of Allāh,	*Bismi'llāhi*
and Allāh is Supremely Great!	*wa 'llāhu Akbar.*
O Allāh, this is from You	*Allāhumma hādha*
and for Your sake!	*min-ka wa la-k.*

It is not recommendable for the slaughtering to be performed by a non-Muslim. If the animal is slaughtered by its owner, that is most meritorious.

The time prescribed for the slaughter begins after the congregational ritual prayer on the Day of the Festival *[Yawm al-ʿĪd]*, and lasts until the end of two of the three Days of *Tashrīq* [Drying Meat].

The person who offers the sacrificial animal should specify its nature, by saying: "This is an *uḍḥiyya*," or: "This is a *hady*." He should also attach a necklace to it, indicating the intended purpose. If he hires a butcher, he should not give him any part of it as his wage.

In accordance with the customary practice, the owner should eat one third of his *uḍḥiyya*, give one third as a personal gift, and donate one third to charity. If he eats more than one third, that is permissible. He is entitled to make use of its skin, but not to sell it or any part of it.

As for the *hady*, if it is voluntary, he is recommended to eat some of it, because the Prophet (Allāh bless him and give him peace) commanded that a piece of meat should be sliced from every *jazūr* [sacrificial camel], and that it should be cooked. He would then eat some of its meat and sup some of its gravy. If the *hady* is obligatory, however, the owner should not eat any part of it, except in the case of the *hady* of *tamattuʿ* and *qirān*.[10]

[10] These terms are explained on p 104.

Chapter

The Sacrifice called *al-ʿAqīqa*

This is a customary practice to celebrate the birth of a child. On the seventh day after the child's birth, two perfectly matched goats are sacrificed on behalf of a boy, and one goat on behalf of a girl. The child's hair is shaved, and its weight in silver is presented as a charitable gift to the poor. If the seventh day is missed, the ceremony is performed on the fourteenth. If that day is also missed, it is performed on the twenty-first. The body of the slaughtered animal should be dismembered without breaking its bones. In all other respects, the *ʿaqīqa* is governed by the same rules as the animal sacrifice made by the pilgrims.

The Book of Commercial Transactions *[Kitāb al-Buyūʿ]*

The Book of Commercial Transactions
[Kitāb al-Buyū']

Allāh (Exalted is He) has said:

Allāh has made trading lawful. *wa aḥalla 'llāhu 'l-bai'a. (2:275)*

Trading is the exchanging of property for property. It is permissible to trade any possession that can be used for some legitimate purpose. The only exception is the dog, for trading it is not permissible, and no fine is imposed on someone who destroys it, because the Prophet (Allāh bless him and give him peace) forbade the setting of a price on the dog.[11]

It is not permissible to trade any item that is not a possession of its vendor, except with the permission of its owner, or when acting as his guardian.

It is also impermissible to trade the following:

- Things that serve no useful purpose, like vermin.
- Things of which the use is unlawful, like alcoholic liquor and *maita* [carrion; meat that has not been ritually slaughtered].
- Things that are not yet in existence, like the future produce of the owner's slave woman or his tree.
- Things of which the identity is unknown, like the fetus [in the slave woman's womb], and the article that is absent, that has not been described, and that has not been seen before the transaction.
- Things that cannot be handed over, like the runaway slave, the horse or camel that has bolted, the birds in the air, and the fish in the water.
- Things that are misappropriated.
- Things that are not singled out, like an unspecified slave from among the owner's slaves, or an unspecified sheep from his flock,

[11] The dog may be used for hunting game. (See p. 261 below).

except when the parts are all of equal value, like a measure of ground wheat.

Subsection

Allāh's Messenger (Allāh bless him and give him peace) forbade the following practices:

- The modes of bargaining called *mulāmasa* [mutual touching], *munābadha* [throwing the article to and fro between the parties] and *bai' al-ḥaṣāt* [concluding the sale by throwing pebbles to each other].
- The trade in which a man outbids his brother.
- The trade in which a townsman acts a broker for a nomad.
- Bidding up the price of an article, without intending to buy it.
- Combining two transactions in one, as when the vendor says: "I have sold you this for ten whole coins or twenty broken coins," or: "I have sold you this on condition that you sell me this, or that you buy this from me."

The Prophet (Allāh bless him and give him peace) also said:

> Do not procure articles of merchandise until the markets drop their prices. If someone buys food, he must not sell it until he has received the full amount.

Chapter

Usury
[Ribā]

As reported by ʿUbāda ibn aṣ-Ṣāmit, Allāh's Messenger (Allāh bless him and give him peace) once said:

> Gold for gold, silver for silver, wheat for wheat, barley for barley, fruit for fruit, and salt for salt, like for like, equal for equal; but if these articles are different, you may trade them however you wish, provided that the transfer of ownership takes place immediately. If someone increases the quantity, or asks for more, he is practicing usury.

It is not permissible to trade an edible commodity—one that is sold by measure or one that is sold by weight—for one of the same species, except in equal quantities. It is not permissible to trade a measured amount thereof for something of the same species that is weighed, nor a weighed amount for a measured amount. If the two species are different, however, it is permissible to trade them on whatever terms are preferred, in an immediate transaction. Postponement is not permissible, nor separation [of the parties] before taking possession, except in the case of the price for the commodity sold for a fixed price.

Whenever two things have a particular name in common, they are one species, unless they are from two different roots. The branches of the species are therefore different species, even if they are all covered by a general term, like *adiqqa* [cereal grains] and *ad'hān* [oils]. It is not permissible to trade one of them that is fresh for one of the same species that is dry, nor one that is pure for one that is mixed, nor one that is raw for one that is cooked.

Allāh's Messenger (Allāh bless him and give him peace) forbade *muzābana*, which is the trading of dried dates for the unripe dates on the tops of date palms. In the case of fresh dates gathered from palm trees, amounting to less than five camel loads, he allowed dried dates to be traded for their conjectural equivalent of dates that are eaten fresh.

Chapter

The Sale of the Roots and the Fruits
[Baiʿ al-Uṣūl wa 'th-Thimār]

The Prophet (Allāh bless him and give him peace) is reported as having said:

> If someone sells a date palm after it has been pollinated, its fruit belongs to the seller, unless the buyer stipulates its inclusion in the sale.

The same rule applies to the sale of any tree, if its fruit is visible. If someone sells land, and on it there is a crop that has been harvested only once, the crop belongs to the seller, unless the buyer stipulates its inclusion in the sale. If it has been reaped time after time, the roots belong to the buyer, and to the seller belongs the crop that is visible at the time of the sale.

Subsection

Allāh's Messenger (Allāh bless him and give him peace) forbade the sale of the fruit [on the tree] until its good quality is apparent. If someone sells the fruit after its good quality has become apparent, on condition that it be left [on the tree] until the harvest, that is permissible. Then, if it is smitten by a blight, it reverts to the seller, because of the saying of Allāh's Messenger (Allāh bless him and give him peace):

> If you sell fruit to your brother, and it is smitten by a blight, it is not lawful for you to receive anything for it. How can you take your brother's property without any right?

The good quality of the fruit of the date palm becomes apparent when it turns red or yellow, that of grapes when they become juicy, and that of other fruits when they show signs of ripeness and taste good.

Chapter

The Option to Revoke
[al-Khiyār]

The two parties have the option to revoke the sale, so long as they have not separated physically. If they separate, and one of them does not rescind the transaction, the transaction is binding, unless it is stipulated that both of them, or one of them, will retain the option for a fixed period of time. They are then bound by their stipulation, even if the period is very long, unless they revoke it.

If one of them discovers some defect in the article he has purchased, and he was not aware of it at the time of the sale, he is entitled to return the article, or to receive compensation for the defect. If the article develops or happens to acquire some increase in value, before he notices the defect, the increase belongs to him, in accordance with the legal maxim *al-kharāj bi'ḍ-ḍamān* [profit goes where the responsibility lies]. If the commodity is ruined, or the slave is emancipated, or returning him is unfeasible, the buyer is entitled to compensation for the defect.

The Prophet (Allāh bless him and give him peace) once said:

> You must not tie the udders of camels and sheep or goats [to prevent their young from sucking them]. If someone buys them after that, he may choose between two options after he has milked them: he may keep them if he finds them satisfactory, or, if he is dissatisfied with them, he may return them together with a measure of fruit. If he notices before milking them that they have had their udders tied, he may return them without anything extra.

The same rule applies to any transaction in which the buyer is swindled, without knowing that he is being swindled: for instance, the seller applies rouge to a slave girl's face, or dyes or curls her hair, or he stores water and releases it over a barren plot of land at the time of showing it to the buyer. Likewise if the seller describes the commodity in a manner that increases its price, and the buyer finds that it does not match his description: for instance, the seller attributes craftsmanship or penmanship to a slave, or describes a riding animal as trotting at a quick and graceful pace, or a cheetah as a fine hunter or a well-trained beast, or a bird as having a sweet voice, and so on. In all such cases, the buyer is entitled to return the commodity.

If the seller informs the buyer of the price of the commodity, and its value then increases, the seller may claim the increase and his share of the profit, if it is a case of *murābaḥa* [a transaction in which it is stipulated that the profit must be divided between the two parties]. If it becomes clear that the seller mistakenly undervalued the commodity, the buyer may choose between two options: he may return it, or he may give him the amount required to make up for his mistake. If it becomes clear that the seller is postponing delivery of the commodity, and he did not inform the buyer of its postponement, the buyer is free to choose between returning it and keeping it.

If the two parties disagree about the amount of the price, they must swear to each other, and each of them is entitled to revoke the transaction, unless he is satisfied with what his companion says.

Chapter

Advance Payment
[as-Salam]

Ibn ʿAbbās (may Allāh be well pleased with him and his father) is reported as having said: "Allāh's Messenger (Allāh bless him and give him peace) arrived in Medina, where they were making payment for fruit one or two years in advance, so he said:

> If someone pays for fruit in advance, let him pay in advance for a fixed measure or a fixed weight, to be delivered on a fixed date.

Advance payment is valid for everything that matches the description exactly, if the seller describes it precisely, mentions its quantity in terms of volume, or weight, or length, or number, and fixes a date for its delivery, and if the buyer gives him the price before the parties separate. Advance payment is also permissible for something to be received in separate parts and at fixed times. If the buyer pays a single price for two things in advance, it is not permissible unless the price of each is clearly distinguished.

If someone pays for a certain thing in advance, he may not transfer the payment to something else. When a commodity has been paid for in advance, it is not permissible to sell it before taking possession of it, nor to transfer it to a third party. It is permissible to revoke the advance payment, or part of it, because revocation *[iqāla]* is a form of annulment *[faskh]*.

Chapter

Lending
[al-Qarḍ]

As reported by Abū Rāfi', Allāh's Messenger (Allāh bless him and give him peace) once borrowed a young camel from a man. Then, when the camels levied for the alms-due were presented to him, he commanded Abū Rāfi' to go and select one with which to reimburse the man for his young camel. Abū Rāfi' came back to him and said: "I could not find any amongst them [that might be suitable], except an excellent camel four cubits in height," so he said:

> Give it to him, for the best of all people is the one who is finest in the settlement of debt.

When someone borrows something, he is obliged to return its equivalent, though it is permissible for him to return something better. He may also borrow separate parts and return a whole item, provided there is no stipulation attached to the loan. If the lender sets a deadline, repayment should not be postponed. It is not permissible for the lender to stipulate something by which he will profit, except when he stipulates a pledge *[rahn]* or a security *[kafīl]*. The lender may not accept a gift from the borrower, unless that was a regular habit of theirs prior to the loan.

Chapter

The Rules of Debt
[Aḥkām ad-Dain]

When payment of a debt is due at the end of a fixed term, the creditor may not demand it before its term has expired, and he may not revoke its term. Payment does not fall due because of the debtor's bankruptcy, nor because of his death, provided that his heirs guarantee it with a pledge or a security. It does fall due before its time, however, if the debtor intends to embarks on a journey, or on a military campaign as a volunteer, so his creditor may prevent him from leaving, unless he receives a guarantee.

If the debt is due immediately from a person in straitened circumstances, he must be granted a delay. If he claims impoverishment, he must swear an oath and thereby obtain relief, unless he is known to have property before that, in which case his word will not be accepted without proof. If he is actually well-to-do, he is obliged to pay the debt in full, and if he refuses, he will be imprisoned until he pays it in full. If his wealth is not sufficient to settle his debt completely, so his creditors ask the judge to prohibit him from using his property freely, he must respond to their request. Then, if the judge prohibits him, it is not permissible for him to dispose of his property, his acknowledgment of responsibility is not accepted, and the judge must take charge of the settlement of his debt. He must begin with anyone who is entitled to the blood money for a crime committed by his slave, so he must provide the victim of the crime with the lesser of two things: the blood money or the value of the criminal. Next in line is anyone who holds a pledge, so must provide him with the lesser of two things: the debt owed to him or the price of his pledge. Where the rest of his debt is concerned, he is entitled to make terms with the creditors.

If someone finds that the commodity he sold for ready money has not suffered any partial damage, and has not been increased by an inseparable addition, and he has not received any part of its price, he is entitled to take possession of it, because of the saying of Allāh's Messenger (Allāh bless him and give him peace):

> If someone sells his commodity for ready money, to a person who is bankrupt, he is more entitled to it than anyone else.

The debtor must distribute the rest of his property among the creditors in proportion to their claims. He must also spend some of his wealth on the bankrupt, and on those whom he is obliged to support, until he has finished the distribution. If a claim is established against him by a witness, and he refuses to swear an oath, his creditors are not required to swear.

Chapter

Transference and Guaranty
[al-Ḥawāla wa 'ḍ-Ḍamān]

If someone's debt is transferred to a person who owes him the same amount, and the latter agrees, the transferor is freed from responsibility. If someone's debt is transferred to person who is solvent, he is obliged to accept the transfer, because of the saying of Allāh's Messenger (Allāh bless him and give him peace):

> If one of you is referred, for the payment of what is owed to him, to a solvent person, let him accept the reference.

If a guarantor provides him with security, the debtor is not freed from responsibility, and the debt becomes incumbent on them both. The creditor is thus entitled to demand payment from whichever of the two he wishes. If he receives the full amount from the one who is ensured, or acquits him of the debt, the guarantor is freed from responsibility. If he acquits the guarantor, however, the actual debtor is not freed from responsibility. If he receives the full amount from the guarantor, the latter may reclaim it from the debtor.

If someone assumes responsibility for the debtor's appearance [to answer a suit in court], but he fails to produce him, he is obliged to pay the debt. If the debtor dies, however, his surety *[kafīl]* is freed from responsibility.

Chapter

Pledging or Pawning
[ar-Rahn]

It is permissible to pledge or pawn anything of which the sale is permissible, and whatever may not be sold may not be pledged or pawned. The transaction does not become binding except by appropriation, which is effected by delivering the pledge, if it is a movable object, or by making it available in other cases. Appropriation by the authorized agent of the pledgee is tantamount to appropriation by the latter in person.

The pledge is a deposit with the pledgee, or with his agent, and he is not accountable for it unless he is guilty of misconduct. The pledgee may not use it for his own benefit, unless it is an animal that can be ridden or milked, in which case he is entitled to ride or milk it in proportion to the fodder he provides.

The pledger is entitled to the profit resulting from its produce, its earnings and its growth, but that is an added pledge. He is responsible for the cost of its maintenance and its storage, and [in the case of a slave] his funeral shroud if he dies. If he damages it, or [if it is a slave] removes it from the pledge by emancipation or *istīlād* [fathering the child of a slave woman], he is obliged to replace it with a pledge of equal value.

If a third party commits a crime against the [slave held as a] pledge, the pledger [not the pledgee] is the litigant [when the case comes to trial], and whatever compensation he receives is a pledge. If the pledge [is a slave and he] commits a crime, the victim of the crime is more entitled to his slave, but if he ransoms him, he is still a pledge.

If the debt falls due, and the pledger does not pay it, the pledge must be sold. The due amount will then be paid from its price, and the remainder will belong to the pledger.

If a sale is made conditional on a pledge or a guarantor, but the pledger refuses to deliver it, and the guarantor refuses to guarantee, the vendor has two options: he may cancel the sale, or he may implement it without a pledge and without a guarantor.

Chapter

Reconciliation
[aṣ-Ṣulḥ]

If someone deducts part of the debt owed to him, or gives his debtor some of the cash that he has in hand, it is permissible, provided he does not make the gift and the exemption conditional on full payment of the rest, or deprive him of his right in any other way, or deduct part of the deferred payment in order to make him pay the rest immediately.

It is permissible for the creditor to demand payment in gold instead of silver, and silver instead of gold, provided he accepts it at its current price, and they conclude their transaction during the session.

If a person claims that another person owes him a debt, but the defendant does not acknowledge his claim, so he becomes reconciled with him on some agreed terms, that is permissible. If one of them is aware of his own falsehood, however, reconciliation is invalid. If someone has a rightful claim against a man, but neither of them knows its actual amount, so they become reconciled with each other, that is permissible.

Chapter

Agency
[Wakāla / Wikāla]

This is permissible in every case where delegation is permissible, so long as the one who appoints and the appointee are both duly qualified. It is a legal contract that is annulled by the death of either one of them, by his violation of it, by his insanity, and by the revocation of his legal competence on account of a lack of sound judgment. The same rules apply to every legal contract, like *shirka/ sharika* [copartnership], *musāqāh* [the watering of trees for a share of their produce], *muzāra'a* [cultivation of land for a share of its produce], *ji'āla / ja'āla / ju'āla* [rewarding], and *musābaqa* [competition].

The agent is not entitled to commission a third party as his agent, nor to purchase from himself, nor to sell to himself, except with the permission of his mandator.

The agent is a trustee who is not responsible for what is damaged, provided that he is not guilty of misconduct, and the word is his word with regard to the damage and the denial of misconduct.

It is permissible to appoint an agent to work for a fixed wage or on some other terms, so the contract is valid if he is told: "Sell this for ten coins, and anything extra is yours."

Chapter

Copartnership
[Shirka/Sharika]

There are four types of copartnership:

1. Copartnership of the reins *[shirkat al-ʿinān]*. This means that the two partners share in what they acquire with their properties and with their bodies.
2. Copartnership of the faces *[shirkat al-wujūh]*. This means that they participate in what they acquire by means of their high-ranking positions.
3. Profit-sharing *[muḍāraba]*. This means that one of the two hands over to the other the goods in which he does not traffic himself, and they share in the profits.
4. Copartnership of the bodies *[shirkat al-abdān]*. This means that they share in whatever legal property they acquire with their bodies, whether by craftsmanship, or harvesting, or hunting and the like, because ʿAbdu'llāh ibn Masʿūd (may Allāh be well pleased with him) is reported as having said: "Saʿd and ʿAmmār and I formed a partnership on the Day of [the Battle of] Badr. Saʿd then came up with two prisoners of war, and neither I nor ʿAmmār came up with anything."

In all of the above, the profit is shared on the basis of what the partners have stipulated, and the loss in proportion to the capital invested. It is not permissible for dirhams [silver coins] to be specified for either partner, nor any specific form of profit. The same rule applies to *musāqāh* [the watering of trees for a share of their produce], *muzāraʿa* [cultivation of land for a share of its produce].

The loss is refunded from the profit. Neither partner may sell his credit, nor take anything from the profit, except with the other's permission.

Chapter

The Watering of Trees for a Share of their Produce *[Musāqāh]* and the Cultivation of Land for a Share of its Produce *[Muzāraʿa]*

Musāqāh [the contract of watering] is permissible in relation to any tree that bears fruit, for a known portion of its fruit, and *muzāraʿa* [the contract of cultivation] is permissible in relation to any plot of land, for a portion of its produce. It does not matter whether the seeds are provided by both parties to the contract, or by only one of them. This is based on the saying of Ibn ʿUmar: "Allāh's Messenger (Allāh bless him and give him peace) employed the people of Khaibar for a share of the crops and fruit produced by the trees and the land." In one version, the wording is: "on condition that they cultivate them at their own expense."

The employee is obliged to perform the work that is normally required. If the employer provides a man with a riding beast on which to work, that is permissible by analogy.

Chapter

The Revival of Uncultivated Land
[Iḥyā' al-Mawāt]

The term *mawāt* is applied to land that is covered with sand and dust blown by the wind, and which is not known to have any owner. If someone revives it, he thereby acquires its ownership, because of the saying of Allāh's Messenger (Allāh bless him and give him peace):

> If someone revives a dead plot of land, it belongs to him.

Its revival signifies its cultivation, by whatever means are suited to the purpose intended, such as building a wall around it and channeling water on to it, if the intention is to sow crops, and uprooting its trees and its rocks, which prevent its being planted and sown. If the reviver digs a well in the land, and strikes water, he acquires possession of the inviolable area surrounding it, which is fifty cubits on every side, if it is an ancient well. If the well was first dug in the time of Islām, its inviolable surrounding area is twenty-five cubits.

Chapter

Rewarding
[Ji'āla / Ja'āla / Ju'āla]

This means that a person says: "If someone returns my lost property, or my stray beast, or if he builds this wall for me, he shall have such-and-such." If someone does that, he is therefore entitled to the reward. This is based on the following traditional report:

According to Abū Sa'īd, a man from among a group of people was stung by a scorpion, so they came to the Companions of Allāh's Messenger (Allāh bless him and give him peace) and said: "Is there a charmer among you?" They replied: "Not until you offer us something as a reward," so they offered them a flock of sheep. One of them thereupon set about reciting the Opening Sūra of the Book *[Fātiḥat al-Kitāb]*, charming and sputtering, until the man recovered. Then they took the sheep. When they asked Allāh's Messenger (Allāh bless him and give him peace) about that, he said:

> How do you know that it is a charm? Take [the reward] and let me share it with you!"

If someone stumbles upon a treasure trove before he learns of the reward, he is not entitled to it.

Chapter

The Treasure Trove
[al-Luqṭa]

There are four types of treasure trove:

1. That which has very little value. It is permissible to take it and make use of it without notification, because of the saying of Jābir: "In the case of the staff, the whip and suchlike, Allāh's Messenger (Allāh bless him and give him peace) granted us a concession, allowing the man who finds it by chance to make use of it."
2. The kind of animal that can protect itself from the smaller beasts of prey, like the camel and the horse, for instance. It is not permissible to take control of such an animal, because the Prophet (Allāh bless him and give him peace) was asked about the stray camel, and he said:

   > What business is it of yours? Leave it alone! It has its hoof, [with which to defend itself], and its stomach, in which to store water and the food it eats from the trees, until its owner comes to it.

   If someone does take control of this kind of animal, he does not become its owner. He is obliged to guarantee its welfare, and he is not relieved of responsibility for it except by handing it over to an agent of the Imām.
3. Things of considerable value, including precious coins, commodities, and the kind of animal that cannot protect itself from the smaller beasts of prey. It is permissible to take control of any such treasure trove, and it must be advertised in the places where people gather, like the markets and the doors of the mosques. Then, when its seeker comes and describes it, the finder must hand it over to him without proof. If it has not been advertised,

it is like the rest of his property, but he cannot dispose of it freely until he advertises its trappings and its quality. Then, when its seeker comes and describes it, he must hand it over to him, or its equivalent if it has already perished. If it is an animal that needs provision, or something that is in danger of perishing, he may eat it before making the advertisement, or sell it and then advertise it, because Zaid ibn Khālid is reported as having said: "Allāh's Messenger (Allāh bless him and give him peace) was asked about the treasure trove of gold and silver, so he said:

> You must advertise its wrapper and its container, and continue to advertise it for a whole year. Then, if its seeker comes some day, you must hand it over to him."

When asked about a sheep, he said:

> Take it, for it belongs to you, or to your brother, or to the wolf!

If the treasure trove perishes during the year of advertisement, without any misconduct on the finder's part, there is no liability for it.

Subsection concerning the Foundling *[al-Laqīṭ]*

The foundling is an abandoned child. The law requires him to be treated as free from slavery and as a Muslim. If any property is found with him, it belongs to him. His guardianship belongs to his finder, provided that he is a Muslim with an honorable record. His maintenance is defrayed from the public treasury, if he has nothing of his own to maintain him. His background is a shadow. If someone claims to be related to him, he will be attached to him, unless he is an unbeliever, in which case he will be attached to him in the context of genealogy, not of religion, and he will not be placed in his custody.

Chapter

Wagering
[as-Sabaq]

Competition without a prize is permissible in all things, but it is not permissible for a prize, except in horse and camel racing and in archery, because of the saying of Allāh's Messenger (Allāh bless him and give him peace):

> There is no wagering except on an arrowhead or the hoof of a camel or horse.

If the prize is awarded by someone other than the two contestants, it is permissible, and it belongs to the winner. If it comes from one of the two contestants, and he wins or the result is a tie, he keeps his wager and is not entitled to anything else. If the other wins, he collects it. If they wager together, it is not permissible unless they insert between them a third contestant, whose horse is comparable to their horses, or his camel to their camels, or his marksmanship to their marksmanship, because of the saying of Allāh's Messenger (Allāh bless him and give him peace):

> If someone inserts a horse between two horses, and he does not feel sure that he will win, it does not constitute a gamble *[qimār]*.

If someone inserts a horse between two horses, and he feels quite sure that he will win, it does constitute a gamble. If he beats them in the race, he will therefore win both their wagers. If one of the other two comes in first, he will keep his own wager and collect his companion's wager.

It is essential to define the contest precisely, to make the goal clear, and [in the case of archery] to determine the target and the number of shots. The archery contest is a matter of hitting the target, not a matter of distance.

Chapter

The Deposit *[al-Wadīʿa]*

The deposit is a trust held by the consignee, who is not subject to any liability for it unless he is guilty of misconduct. He is liable for it, however, in any of the following cases:

- If he does not keep it in a safe place along with similar items, or in the kind of safe place in which he is instructed to keep it.
- If he makes use of it for his own purposes.
- If he mixes it with something from which it cannot be distinguished.
- If he removes it in order to do business with it, and then replaces it.
- If he breaks the seal of its container.
- If he disclaims it and then acknowledges it.
- If he refuses to return it when it is requested, despite the fact that its return is possible.

If he says: "You did not entrust me," and then claims that it has perished or been returned, his claim is not accepted. If he says: "I have nothing belonging to you," and then claims that it has has perished or been returned, his claim is accepted.

[Unlike the deposit], the loan *[ʿāriya]* is guaranteed, even if the borrower does not mistreat it.

The Book of Hiring and Leasing
[Kitāb al-Ijāra]

The Book of Hiring and Leasing
[Kitāb al-Ijāra]

Hiring or leasing is a contract relating to utilities. It is binding on both parties, neither of whom has the right to revoke it, and it is not annulled by his death or his insanity. It is annulled by the perishing of the commodity that is the subject of the contract, or by the termination of its usefulness. The leaseholder is entitled to annul the contract because of a defect in the commodity, whether the defect is ancient or recent.

A contract of hire or lease is not valid unless its usufruct is determined, either by common knowledge, like the occupation of a house, or by description, like the tailoring of a particular garment, or the building of a wall, or the transporting of something to a particular place. If the contract refers to a specific object, its precise definition is essential.

If someone takes a lease on something, he is entitled to substitute another person for himself, if the substitute reimburses him for the cost of his lease, or provides him with something of equal or lesser value.

If someone hires a plot of land for the purpose of cultivating a particular crop, he is entitled to cultivate one that is less troublesome. If he cultivates one that is more troublesome, he is obliged to pay the corresponding rate of hire.

If someone hires a beast in order to ride to a certain place, and he travels beyond it, or in order to transport a certain load, and he adds to it, he is obliged to pay the corresponding fee for the increase, and he is held accountable for the commodity if it perishes. He incurs no liability, however, if it perishes without any malpractice on his part.

As for the hireling who hires himself out for a specific period of time, he is not held accountable for anything that perishes in his hand without any negligence on his part. No liability is incurred by a cupper, or a circumciser, or a physician, provided that he is known for his skill in the craft, and their hands do not cause injury, nor by the shepherd, so long as he does not behave improperly. As for the bleacher and the tailor, and other such craftsmen, they are held accountable for anything that is ruined by their work, but not for something that perishes in their custody.

Chapter

Misappropriation, Usurpation
[Ghaṣb]

If a person has misappropriated something, he is obliged to return it. He must also pay the regular fee for hiring such an article, if he has the amount due for the period in which it was at his disposal. If he has less, he is obliged to compensate for the shortfall.

If a misappropriated slave commits a crime, the blood money for his crime is incumbent on the usurper, whether he commits it against his master or a stranger. If a stranger commits a crime against the misappropriated slave, his master is entitled to hold responsible whichever of the two he wishes [either the usurper or the stranger].

If the misappropriated item increases in value, the usurper must return it with its increase, whether the addition is inseparable or separable. If it increases or decreases, he must return it with its increase and hold himself responsible for the decrease, whether the difference results from his action or from some other cause. If he carves a piece of wood to make a door, or works on a bar of iron to fashion needles, he must return them with their increased value, and hold himself responsible for any decrease in their value. The same rule applies in cases like the following:

- He misappropriates some cotton wool and spins it, or a piece of yarn and weaves it, or a garment and bleaches it, or takes it apart and stitches it.
- He misappropriates some seeds and they become crops, or some date stones and they become trees, or some eggs and they become chickens.

If he misappropriates a slave, and he increases in his physique or because of his training, but the increase then departs, the usurper must return him and the value of the increase.

If the misappropriated item perishes, or its return is unfeasible, the usurper is liable for its equivalent, if it is a commodity that is measured or weighed, and for its price if it is not like that. If he then becomes able to return it, he should return it and receive the price.

If he mixes the misappropriated item with something that is indistinguishable from it, he is obliged to return its equivalent from the mixture. If he mixes it with something of a different kind, he is obliged to its return its equivalent from wherever he wishes.

If he misappropriates a plot of land and then plants trees on it, he must uproot what he has planted, return the land, provide compensation for its loss of value, and pay its rent. If he cultivates it and reaps the crop, the usurper must return the land and pay its rent. If its owner becomes aware of the crop before its harvesting, he is free to choose between that and taking the crop for its price.

If someone misappropriates a slave girl, then has sexual intercourse with her and makes her bear a child, he is subject to the legal penalty [for sexual misconduct]. He must also return her and her child to her owner, provide the dower appropriate to a woman of her kind, compensate for her loss of value, and pay the fee for hiring a slave like her. If he sells her and the buyer has sexual intercourse with her—without knowing that she is misappropriated—the buyer is liable for her dower, her price and that of her child, and the fee for hiring a slave like her, all of which he may reclaim from the usurper.

Chapter

The Right of Preemption
[Shufʿa]

The right of preemption *[shufʿa]* is a person's entitlement to wrest his partner's share from the hand of its buyer. It is subject to seven preconditions:

1. Sale. It does not apply to a gift, nor to a pious endowment, nor to compensation for a *khulʿ* [divorce at the instance of the wife],[12] nor to a bridal dower.
2. The preempted share must consist of immovable property, or something connected with building and cultivation.
3. It must be an undivided property. As for that which is divided by fixed boundaries, there is no right of preemption where it is concerned, because of the saying of Jābir: "Allāh's Messenger (Allāh bless him and give him peace) decreed preemption in the case of any property that is not divided. There is no right of preemption, therefore, when the boundaries have been fixed and the roads have been turned in different directions."
4. It must be divisible. As for property that is indivisible, there is no right of preemption where it is concerned.
5. The preemptor must take the whole share. If he demands only part of it, his right of preemption is therefore annulled. If there are two preemptors, the right of preemption is held by them both, in proportion to their shares. If one of them refrains from exercising his right of preemption, the other has no option except taking the whole or abstaining.

[12] See p. 224 below.

6. The ability to pay the price. If the preemptor is incapable of paying it, or part of it, his right of preemption is annulled. If the price is fungible, he must pay its equivalent, and if it is not fungible, he must pay its value. If the two parties disagree about its amount, and neither of them has proof, the word is the word of the buyer together with his oath.
7. The claim must be made immediately, as soon as the preemptor knows of the transaction. If he postpones it, his right of preemption is therefore annulled, unless he is incapable of making his claim because of absence, or imprisonment, or sickness, or juvenility, in which case he may exercise his right of preemption when he becomes able to do so. His right of preemption is annulled, however, if he is capable of having his claim witnessed, but he fails to do so. If he does not come to know of the transaction until three or more parties have bought and sold with one another, he is entitled to claim from whichever of them he wishes. If he takes from the first, the second may reclaim what the first took from him, and the third may reclaim what the second took from him. When he takes the property, and it has on it a plantation or a building belonging to the buyer, the preemptor must give him its price, unless the buyer prefers to uproot it without causing damage. If it has on it crops or visible fruits belonging to the buyer, they should be left until the harvest or the gathering.

If someone buys an immovable property and a sword in a single contract, the preemptor is entitled to take the immovable property exclusively.

The Book of Endowment
[Kitāb al-Waqf]

The Book of Endowment
[Kitāb al-Waqf]

The term *waqf* signifies the inalienable endowment of the root, and the dedication of the fruit to charitable purposes. It is permissible in the case of any article of which the sale is permissible, and from which benefit will always be derived, because of its permanent nature. It is not valid in the case of anything other than that, such as coins, foodstuffs and perfumes. It is not valid unless it is dedicated to a pious or charitable purpose, as indicated by the following traditional report:

ʿUmar said: "O Messenger of Allāh, in my opinion, the property I gained at Khaibar is more precious than any property I have ever obtained. What do you command me to do with it?" He received the reply:

> If you wish, you may endow its root and dedicate its fruit to charitable purposes, with the provision that its root must not be sold, nor donated, nor bequeathed as inheritance.

ʿUmar therefore dedicated it to charity, for the sake of the poor, needy relatives, slaves, the cause of Allāh, the traveler and the guest.

No sin is committed if its administrator eats of it in moderation, or feeds a friend, provided that he does not enrich himself from it.

The validity of the endowment is established by verbal statement, and also by action that proves it, such as building a mosque and giving the call to prayer therein, or constructing a watering place and making it available to the people. Its sale is not permissible, unless its usufructs are completely exhausted, it which case it should be sold and the proceeds used to purchase a replacement for it. If a horse that has been endowed is unfit for military expedition, it should be sold and the proceeds used to purchase something useful for the holy war *[jihād]*. If a mosque serves no useful purpose in its location, it should be sold and transferred to a place where it provides benefit.

Deference must be paid to the intention of the founder, with regard to the endowment, its expenditure, its prerequisites and its organization. His wishes must also be consulted with regard to the inclusion and exclusion of beneficiaries, as well as the qualification of the administrator and his maintenance. If the founder assigns the endowment to the offspring of so-and-so, then to the needy, the males and the females are equally entitled, unless he gives preference to some of them. If none of the offspring survive, the endowment belongs to the needy.

If the endowment is assigned to all those who can possibly be included, it is necessary to include them all, and to treat them equally, unless the founder gives preference to some of them. If their total inclusion is impossible, it is permissible to prefer some of them over others, and to allot it to one of them exclusively.

Chapter

The Deed of Gift
[al-Hiba]

This is the transfer of the ownership of property, during life, without any exchange. It is validated by offer and acceptance, and by presentation combined with evidence of its nature. It becomes binding upon receipt. Its retraction is not permissible, except in the case of the father, because of the saying of Allāh's Messenger (Allāh bless him and give him peace):

> It is not lawful for anyone to give a gift and then retract it, except when the gift is given by the parent to his offspring.

In the giving of gifts to offspring, the law requires that they be treated fairly in proportion to their inheritance, because of the saying of Allāh's Messenger (Allāh bless him and give him peace):

> Practice true devotion to Allāh, and treat you offspring equitably.

If someone says to a man: "I have assigned my house to you for life," or, "It is yours as a gift for life," it belongs to him and to his heirs after him. If he tells him: "Its habitation is yours for your lifetime," he may take possession of it whenever he wishes.

Chapter

The Sick Person's Donation
[ʿAṭiyat al-Marīḍ]

As for the donations made by a sick person who is in danger of dying from his sickness, or by someone whose life is in similar danger—like a soldier standing between the ranks when battle is joined, and one who is sent forward to be killed, or the sailor on the stormy sea, or someone whose town is visited by the plague—such donations are governed by six of the rules that apply to the testamentary bequest *[waṣiyya]*,[13] namely:

1. If made to a stranger, the donation is not permissible in excess of one third [of the donor's property], and if made to an heir, it is not permissible except with the consent of the other heirs. This rule is based on a traditional report, according to which a man emancipated six slaves at the time of his death, when he owned no property apart from them, so the Prophet (Allāh bless him and give him peace) sent for them, divided their number by three, then emancipated two of them and enslaved the other four.
2. In keeping with the traditional report, freedom should be granted to one of the slaves by casting lots, if their total number is not divisible by three.
3. If he emancipates a slave without specific identification, or with an identification that is ambiguous, the selection should be made by casting lots.
4. It is necessary to consider whether the donation came from one third of the donor's estate at the time of death. If he emancipated or donated a slave when he owned no other property, but then

[13] See p. 169 below.

came to possess twice his value at the time of death, we should conclude that the slave was wholly emancipated at the time of his emancipation, and that what the donor acquired after that belonged to the donor. On the other hand, if he incurred a debt that would consume his acquisition entirely, no part of the slave would be emancipated, and his donation would be invalid. If he bequeathed something, but the legatee did not receive it for some time, it would be valued at the time of the legator's death, not at the time of receipt.

5. In order to determine whether he [the donee] is an heir, it is necessary to consider the state of affairs at the time of death. If someone makes a donation or a bequest to his brother, when he [the donor or legator] has no children, and a son is born to him [after his death], the donation and the bequest are both valid, but if he had a son and then died, both would be null and void.
6. Where both [the donation and the bequest] are concerned, no consideration is given to the refusal and consent of the heirs, except after the death [of the donor or legator].

The donation is different from the bequest where these four rules are concerned:

1. The donation is effective immediately. If someone emancipates a slave, he thus becomes a free man, and if he donates a slave to a person, the donee becomes his owner and his earnings belong to him. On the other hand, if he bequeathes him, the legatee does not become his owner until after the legator's death, and if he makes his emancipation conditional on his liberator's death, he is not emancipated until that time. Whatever he earns in the meantime belongs to the heirs, and so does any separable element that happens to augment his value.
2. In the case of the donation, its acceptance and its rejection take effect immediately. In the case of the bequest, on the other hand, its acceptance and its rejection are irrelevant except after the death of the legator.
3. The donation is binding, so the donor has no right to retract it, whereas the legator is entitled to retract the bequest whenever he wishes.

4. The donor is entitled to make various donations to one person after another, so long as their total does not amount to more than one third of his property. In the case of the bequest, on the other hand, the legator must bequeath the same amount to the each legatee, from the first to the last. He must allocate any loss of value to each one in proportion to his bequest, whether or not it includes emancipation. The same rule applies to donations, if they are made simultaneously.

The Book of Testamentary Bequests *[Kitāb al-Waṣāyā]*

The Book of Testamentary Bequests
[Kitāb al-Waṣāyā]

Sa'd is reported as having said: "I said: 'O Messenger of Allāh, hard work has brought me to the point you observe. I am wealthy, and I have no one to inherit from me except a daughter. Should I donate two thirds of my wealth to charity?' He said: 'No!' I said: 'One half?' He said: 'No!' I said: 'One third?' He said:

One third, for one third is a very great deal. That you should leave your heirs rich is better than that you should leave them poor, reduced to begging from other people."

When someone leaves wealth or property, he is recommended to bequeath one fifth of his estate. The bequeathing of property and *tadbīr* [the promise of emancipation for a slave after his master's death] are both valid when made by anyone whose deed of gift *[hiba]* is valid, and also by the minor of sound mind and the spendthrift, whose freedom to dispose of his property is otherwise restricted.

The bequest is valid when made in favor of anyone in whose favor the deed of gift is valid, and also in favor of the child in the womb, if he is known to exist at the time of the bequest in his favor. It is valid when it consists of anything that may be used for a legal purpose, like the hunting dog and sheep or goats. It is also valid when it consists of impurities that serve some useful purpose, and of something that has not yet come into existence, like the child in the womb of the legator's slave woman, or the future produce of his tree. It is also valid when it consists of any of the following:

- Something that cannot be delivered by the legator, like birds in the air and fish in the water.
- Something that he does not possess, like one hundred silver coins that are not in his possession.
- Something that is not specifically identified, like a slave from

among his slaves. (The heirs may then give the legatee whichever of them they wish.)

- Something of unknown quantity, like a portion or a part of his property. (The heirs may then give the legatee whatever they wish.)

Subsection

If the testamentary bequest *[waṣiyya]* is annulled, in whole or in part, it reverts to the heirs. Consider the following examples:

If the testator decrees that the slave of Zaid should be bought for one hundred coins and thereby emancipated, but the slave dies, or his owner does not sell him, the hundred coins belong to the heirs.

If he bequeaths one hundred coins to be spent on a *faras ḥabīs* [a horse to be used by warriors in the sacred cause], but the horse dies, the money belongs to the heirs.

If he bequeaths one thousand coins to enable Zaid to perform the Pilgrimage, but he does not perform the Pilgrimage, the money belongs to the heirs. If the legatee says: "Give me more than the cost of the Pilgrimage," he will not be given anything.

If the legatee dies before the death of the legator, or he rejects the bequest, it reverts to the heirs.

If he makes a bequest to a living person and one who is dead, the living person is entitled to half of the bequest.

If he bequeaths one third of his estate to his heir and to a stranger, the stranger is entitled to one sixth, and the heir's sixth is dependent on the approval [of the other heirs].

Chapter

The Executor
[al-Mūṣā ilai-h]

It is permissible for the testator to appoint any Muslim of sound mind and honest reputation, whether male or female, as an executor responsible for any action that would be permissible for the testator, such as settling his debts, distributing his bequest, and considering the interest of his infant children.

When he assigns to his executor the guardianship of his children who are infants or lunatics, his guardianship over them is established, and he may manage their property in any way that is to their advantage, such as buying and selling, receiving what is given to them, spending a reasonable amount on them and on what is necessary for their support, trading on their behalf, and investing their wealth for part of the profit. If he does business for them personally, he is not entitled to any share of the profit, but he is entitled to consume some of their property when necessary, to the extent required by his work, and he incurs no penalty thereby. He may not consume [any of their property] if he is rich, however, because of the saying of Allāh (Exalted is He):

Whoever is rich, let	*wa man kāna ghaniyyan;*
him abstain generously	*fa-'l-yasta'fif:*
and whoever is poor let	*wa man kāna faqīran*
him consume in reason. (4:6)	*fa-l'-ya'kul bi'l-ma'rūf.*

The executor is not entitled to delegate the responsibility that has been assigned to him, nor to buy and sell anything from their property for his own benefit. That is permissible only for the father, so no one may have absolute control of the property of the minor and the lunatic, except the father, or his authorized agent, or the governor.

Subsection

The guardian is entitled to permit a discerning minor to act independently, in order to put his discretion to the test. What is meant here by "discretion *[rushd]*" is competence in dealing with property. Then, if he sees evidence of his discretion, he should deliver his property to him when he reaches puberty. This is equally applicable to a male or a female. If the young person reverts to childish incompetence, the guardian should reimpose restriction on him. No one should supervise his property except the legal authority, and the restriction should not be released from him except by his decree. His acknowledgment is not acceptable in relation to property, but it is acceptable in relation to legal penalties *[ḥudūd]*, retaliation *[qiṣāṣ]*, and divorce by repudiation *[ṭalāq]*. If he repudiates [a wife] or emancipates [a slave], his repudiation is therefore effective, but not his emancipation.

Subsection

If the owner permits his slave to engage in trade, his buying and selling and his acknowledgment are valid, but his independent action is effective only to the extent of the permission granted to him. If his owner or his guardian sees him acting independently, and does not forbid him to do so, this does not amount to his having been granted permission.

The Book of the Shares of Inheritance *[Kitāb al-Farāʾiḍ]*

The Book of the Shares of Inheritance *[Kitāb al-Farāʾiḍ]*

The *farāʾiḍ* are the apportioned shares of the *mīrāth* [inheritance]. The *wārith* [heir] inherits as one of the following three: (1) *dhū farḍ* [quota-heir]; (2) *ʿaṣaba* [relative who qualifies as a residuary]; (3) *dhū raḥim* [distant relative].

The quota-heirs are ten in number: (1,2) the two spouses; (3,4) the two parents; (5) the paternal grandfather; (6) the grandmother; (7) the daughters; (8) the son's daughters; (9) the sisters; (10) the brothers on the mother's side.

The widower is entitled to one half of the inheritance, except when his deceased wife has children, in which case he is entitled to one quarter. If the deceased husband leaves only one widow, she is entitled to one quarter, and if he leaves more than one—up to the maximum of four [permitted by Islāmic law]—they share that quarter equally. If he has children, however, the widows are entitled to one eighth [to be shared equally].

Subsection

The father's entitlement is different in each of three situations: (1) In the presence of male descendants of the deceased, he is entitled to one sixth [as a *dhū farḍ*]. (2) In the absence of male descendants of the deceased, he inherits as a residuary *[ʿaṣaba]*. (3) In the presence of female descendants of the deceased, he inherits in both capacities.

Subsection

The paternal grandfather's entitlement is like that of the father, in the three situations mentioned above, but there may also be a fourth: In the presence of full or paternal brothers and sisters of the deceased, he is entitled to receive the most favorable fraction of their share, like a brother, or to receive one third of the whole estate. If they are accompanied by a *dhū farḍ*, the latter receives his quota, then the paternal grandfather is entitled to the most favorable fraction of their share, or one third of the remainder, or one sixth of the whole estate.

Full and paternal siblings are alike in this respect, if those left by the deceased are of one kind only. If they are of both kinds, the full siblings share with the grandfather and the paternal siblings, then receive their shares of the residue, unless the only full sibling is a sister, in which case she receives one half, and the remainder belongs to the paternal siblings. If only one sixth remains beyond the quota, the grandfather receives it and the brothers are precluded.

These rules do not apply in what is called the "perplexing" problem *[al-akdariyya]*, which occurs when the deceased leaves a husband, a mother, a sister and a grandfather. The husband is entitled to one half, the mother to one third, the grandfather to one sixth, and the sister to one half. The sister's half and the grandfather's sixth are therefore proportionately reduced. The grandfather's quota-share is not reduced in any other case, and this is the only case in which a sister is entitled to a quota-share together with a grandfather. If there is no husband, the mother is entitled to one third, and the remainder is divided proportionately between the sister and the grandfather. This is called the "awkward" problem *[al-kharqāʾ]*, because it was the subject of considerable disagreement among the Companions (may Allāh be well pleased with them). If they are accompanied by a paternal brother or sister, the shares may be apportioned on the basis of division into fifty-fourths, in accordance with what is called "Zaid's abbreviated solution *[mukhtaṣara Zaid]*." If they are accompanied by another paternal brother, the apportionment may be based on division into ninetieths, in accordance with what is called "Zaid's ninety-part solution *[tisʿīniyya Zaid]*." There is no disagreement concerning the exclusion of maternal brothers and the sons of brothers.

Subsection

The mother's entitlement is different in each of four situations: (1) In the presence of children, or two or more brothers and sisters, she is entitled to one sixth. (2) In the presence of the father and the husband or wife, she is entitled to one third of the residue after deducting the quota-share of the husband or wife. (3) In other [normal] situations, she is entitled to one third of the whole estate. (4) If her child was disowned [by her husband] through *liʿān* [divorce by mutual cursing],[14] or was a child of adultery *[walad zinā]*, she inherits as an *ʿaṣaba* [not as a quota-sharer]. In her absence, her *ʿaṣaba* relatives inherit as *ʿaṣaba*.

Subsection

As for the grandmother [or great-grandmother, in any degree of ascent]—in the absence of a mother—she is entitled to one sixth. If there are more than one of them in the same degree, the sixth is divided equally among them. If some of them are nearer in degree than others, the sixth belongs to those who are nearest. The grandmother inherits even when her son is alive. The only grandmothers [and great-grandmothers] entitled to inherit are: the mother's mother, the father's mother, the mother of the paternal grandfather, and the mothers of these in any degree of ascent. A [great-] grandmother does not inherit if she is related to the deceased through a father of a mother's mother, nor through a father higher in degree than the paternal grandfather. If the deceased leaves both of his mother's grandmothers and both of his father's grandmothers, the mother of his father's mother is precluded, and the inheritance belongs to the remaining three.

[14] See p. 247 below.

Subsection

The daughter is entitled to one half, and two or more daughters are entitled to two-thirds [divided between or among them]. In the absence of daughters, the son's daughters take their place. In their presence, however, the son's daughters are precluded, unless they are accompanied by a male descendant in the same or a lower degree, in which case they share the residue with him as *ʿaṣaba*. If there is one daughter and one or more son's daughters, the daughter is entitled to one half, and one sixth belongs to the son's daughter or daughters—adding up to the two-thirds [allotted to two or more daughters]—unless they are accompanied by a male, in which case they share the residue with him as *ʿaṣaba*.

Subsection

Full sisters are like daughters where their quota-shares are concerned. Paternal sisters in the company of full sisters are like the son's daughters in the company of daughters, and only in their brother's presence do they inherit as *ʿaṣaba*. Sisters in the company of daughters share the residue as *ʿaṣaba*, and they are not entitled to a prescribed quota, because of the saying of Ibn Masʿūd (may Allāh be well pleased with him) concerning the combination of a daughter, a son's daughter and a sister: "In this case, my judgment is that of Allāh's Messenger (Allāh bless him and give him peace), so the daughter receives one half, the son's daughter receives one sixth, and the residue belongs to the sister.

Subsection

Maternal siblings are equal in their entitlement, whether they are male or female. One of them is entitled to one sixth, and two are entitled to two-sixths. If they are more than that, they are sharers in the third.

Chapter

Preclusion from Inheritance
[al-Ḥajb]

The full sibling is precluded by three relatives of the deceased: (1) the son, (2) the son's son, and (3) the father. The paternal sibling is precluded by these three, and also by the full brother. The maternal sibling is precluded by four relatives of the deceased: (1) the children, whether male or female, (2) the son's children, (3) the father, and (4) the paternal grandfather. The paternal grandfather is precluded by the father, and every great-grandfather by one who is more closely related to the deceased.

Chapter

The Residuary Heirs
[al-ʿAṣabāt]

These include every male who is related to the deceased, either directly or through another male, with the exception of the husband. They also include the *muʿtiqa* [female emancipator of a slave] and her *ʿaṣabāt*.

The one most entitled to inherit is the one who is most closely related to the deceased, in the following order of priority:

- The son, then the son's son, and then the next in line of descent.
- The father, then the father's father in any degree of ascent, so long as there are no brothers.
- The father's sons, then their sons, in any degree of descent.
- The sons of the paternal grandfather, then their sons.

The sons of a father who is higher [in the line of ascent] do not inherit in the presence of the sons of a father who is lower, however far down the line. Of all the son's of a father, the one most entitled to inherit is the one most closely related to the deceased. If their degrees are the same, the one most entitled is the one who is related through both parents.

Four of the *ʿaṣābāt* cause their sisters to inherit with them as residuaries [in accordance with the Qurʾānic revelation]:

To the male the equivalent of the portion of two females. (4:11)	*li'dh-dhakari mithlu ḥaẓẓi 'l-unthayain.*

They are: (1) the son, (2) the son's son, (3) the full brother, and (4) the paternal brother. As for the other *ʿaṣābāt*, their inheritance is confined to the males, like the sons of the sister, and the paternal uncles and their sons.

If a residuary *[ʿaṣāba]* is the only heir, he inherits the whole of the estate. If he is accompanied by a quota-heir *[dhū farḍ]*, the latter receives his quota first of all, and the remainder belongs to the residuary, because of the saying of Allāh's Messenger (Allāh bless him and give him peace):

> Allot the quota-shares to those entitled to them, then whatever remains will belong to the male who is first in priority.

If the quota-shares account for the whole estate, the residuary heir is precluded, as when the deceased leaves a husband, a mother, maternal brothers, and full brothers. The husband is then entitled to one half, the mother to one sixth, and the maternal brothers to one third, so the full brothers are precluded. This case is called *al-mushtaraka* [the shared quota] and *al-ḥimāriyya* [the asinine].[15] If they were sisters instead of brothers, they would be entitled to two-thirds, the shares would be proportionately reduced, and the case would be called *umm al-furūkh* [the mother of the chickens].

If the child is a *khunthā* [hermaphrodite], the point of urination should be examined. If the urine is discharged from the male organ, the hermaphrodite inherits as a man, and if it is discharged from the female organ, as a woman. If the urine is discharged from both organs equally, the gender is ambiguous, so the hermaphrodite is entitled to half of the inheritance of a male and half of the inheritance of a female. The same rule applies to blood money, compensation for wounds, and other payments due to the hermaphrodite, and such a person is never allowed to marry.

[15] In a case of this kind, the Caliph ʿUmar (may Allāh be well pleased with him) assigned the quota-share of one third to the maternal brothers, and nothing to the full brothers, so they said: "O Commander of the Believers, suppose that our father was an ass *[ḥimār]*, and let us share by reason of our mother's relationship!" He then decided that the quota should be shared *[mushtaraka]* by all the brothers.

Chapter

Distant Relatives
[Dhawu 'l-Arḥām]

The *dhawu 'l-arḥām* are all those kinsfolk who not related to the deceased as residuaries, nor as quota-heirs. They are not entitled to any inheritance in the presence of a residuary *[ʿaṣaba]* or a quota-heir *[dhū farḍ]*, with the exception of one of the spouses, for they are entitled to what remains after the spouse's share, with no preclusion and no reduction.

They inherit according to proximity of degree, so each individual among them is placed in the position of the relative through whom he or she is connected to the deceased. The children of the daughters of the son's daughters, and of the sisters, are therefore in the position of their mothers. The daughters of the brothers and the paternal uncles, and the sons of the maternal brothers, are like their fathers. The paternal aunts, and the paternal uncles on the mother's side, are like the father. The maternal uncles, the maternal aunts, and the mother's father, are like the mother.

If there are two or more of them from a single line of connection, the one most entitled is the one most closely related to the heir [who would have inherited if alive]. If they are equally close, the estate is divided among the heirs through whom they are related, and the share of each heir is assigned to those related through him or her. The males and the females are equally entitled, if their lines of connection to the deceased are equal. If the deceased leaves a son of a daughter, a daughter of another daughter, and a son and a daughter of another daughter, the estate is divided among the daughters in three thirds, then assigned to their children: one third to the son, one third to the daughter, and the remaining third to the other son and daughter, divided in half between the two. If he leaves three separate paternal aunts, and three separate maternal aunts, one third is divided among the maternal aunts, and two thirds among the paternal aunts.

If the *dhawu 'l-arḥām* are related to the deceased by different lines, each distant relative must trace his or her connection to the heir [who would have inherited if alive], and the estate will then be divided in the manner we have described. The lines of connection are three: filiation *[bunuwwa]*, maternity *[umūma]* and paternity *[ubuwwa]*.

Chapter

The Basic Elements of the Arithmetical Problems *[Uṣūl al-Masā'il]*

There are seven of these:

1. If the quota-share is one half, the arithmetical divisor is two. (1/2)
2. If the quota-shares are one third and two thirds, the divisor is three. (1/3+2/3)
3. If the quota-share is one quarter, either alone or in conjunction with one half, the divisor is four. (1/4 ; 1/4+2/4)
4. If the quota-share is one eighth, either alone or in conjunction with one half, the divisor is eight. (1/8 ; 1/8+4/8)

There is no fractional reduction *['awl]* in the four cases listed above.

5. If the quota-shares are one half plus one third or two thirds or one sixth, the divisor is six. When fractional reduction is necessary, the sixths are reduced to tenths.
6. If the quota-shares are one quarter plus one of these three [one third or two thirds or one sixth], the divisor is twelve. When fractional reduction is necessary, the twelfths are reduced to seventeenths.
7. If the quota-shares are one eighth plus one sixth or two thirds, the divisor is twenty-four. When fractional reduction is necessary, the twenty-fourths are reduced to twenty-sevenths.

Chapter

Reversion
[ar-Radd]

If the quota-shares do not account for the whole estate, and there is no residuary heir *[ʿaṣaba]*, the remainder reverts to them in proportion to their quotas, with the exception of the spouses. If one of the spouses is with them, he or she receives the share to which he or she is normally entitled, then the remainder is divided among those entitled to the reversion.

In any case where a residuary *[ʿaṣaba]* inherits, there is no fractional reduction *[ʿawl]* and no reversion *[radd]*.

Chapter

Impediments to Inheritance
[Mawāniʿ al-Mīrāth]

There are three impediments to inheritance:

1. Difference of religion *[dīn]*. Members of one *milla* [religious community] do not inherit from members of another *milla*, because of the sayings of Allāh's Messenger (Allāh bless him and give him peace):

   > The Muslim does not inherit from the unbeliever *[kāfir]*, nor the unbeliever from the Muslim.

The members of two different religious communities do not inherit from one another. The apostate *[murtadd]* does not inherit from anyone, and if he dies, his property is booty *[faiʾ]*.

2. Slavery. The slave does not inherit from anyone, and he possesses no property to be inherited. If someone is partly free, however, he does inherit and his heirs inherit from him. He precludes [less qualified heirs] in proportion to the freedom with which he is endowed.[16]
3. Killing. The killer does not inherit from the person who is killed without a legal right. If he kills him with a legal right, like killing in the execution of a legal penalty *[ḥadd]* or in retaliation *[qiṣāṣ]*, or the just man's killing of the rebel insurgent,[17] his inheritance is not impeded.

[16] Se the Chapter headed "Preclusion from Inheritance *[al-Ḥajb]*" on p. 179 above.

[17] See the Chapter headed "Fighting against Rebel Insurgents *[Qatl Ahl al-Baghy]*" on p. 308 below.

Chapter

Various Problems
[Masā'il Shattā]

If someone dies leaving a child in the womb as his heir, you should withhold the inheritance of two males, if their inheritance adds up to more [than that of the child], and if not, the inheritance of any two. You should give each heir the amount that is certain [in any case], and withhold the rest until it is clear [after the birth of the child].

If one of the heirs is missing and nothing is known of his whereabouts, you should give each heir the amount that is certain [in any case], and withhold the rest until his condition is known, unless he is lost in a dangerous place, or beyond the reach of his people, in which case you should wait for four years and then distribute [his share of the inheritance].

If a sick person divorces his wife during an illness that is expected to be fatal, with a repudiation by which he is suspected of intending to exclude her from the inheritance, her inheritance is not annulled so long as she is in the *ʿidda* [period of waiting before the divorce becomes final]. If the divorce is revocable, the two spouses inherit from each other during the *ʿidda*, whether in health or in sickness.

If all the heirs acknowledge that someone is entitled to share with them in the inheritance, and he believes them, or he is a minor of unknown relationship, his relationship and his inheritance are established. If one of them acknowledges him, his relationship is not established, and he is only entitled to the excess of the inheritance of the heir who acknowledges him.

Chapter

The Relationship of Patronage *[al-Walāʾ]*

Patronage belongs to the one who emancipates [a slave], because of the saying of Allāh's Messenger (Allāh bless him and give him peace):

> Patronage belongs only to the one who emancipates.

If the slave is emancipated by kinship, or *kitāba* [a written contract by which the slave becomes free on the payment of a certain sum to his master], or *tadbīr* [the promise of freedom upon the master's death], or *istīlāʾ* [capture from an enemy], the emancipator has patronage over him. He also has patronage over his children from a free woman who has been emancipated, or a female slave, and over the emancipated slaves of his emancipated slaves, and the emancipated slaves of his children and their children, however far down the line of descent. He inherits from them provided there is no one who precludes him from their inheritance, then his residuary heirs *[ʿaṣābāt]* inherit from them after him.

Suppose someone says: "Emancipate your slave on my behalf, and I shall be responsible for his price." If the owner acts accordingly, the person who gives the command is obliged to pay his price, and he is entitled to his patronage. If he does not say "on my behalf," he is responsible for the price, but the patronage belongs to the emancipator. If someone emancipates his slave on behalf of a living person, without his command, or on behalf of a dead person, the patronage belongs to the emancipator. If he emancipates him on his behalf at his command, the patronage belongs to the emancipator on his behalf at his command.

If one of the two free spouses is free by origin, there is no patronage over their child. If one of the two is a slave, the children follow the mother in her freedom or her slavery. If the mother is a slave, her children are therefore slaves belonging to her master. If he emancipates them, he is entitled to their patronage, and he does not lose it in any situation. If the father is a slave and the mother has been emancipated, her children are free and the patronage over them belongs to their mother's patron.

If the owner emancipates his slave, his patronage over him is established and the patronage of his children is attached to him. If he [the emancipated slave] buys his father, the latter is thereby emancipated, and he is entitled to his patronage and the patronage of his brothers.

Chapter

Inheritance through Patronage *[al-Mīrāth bi'l-Walā']*

Patronage is not transmitted by bequest, and the nearest of the residuary heirs *['aṣabāt]* of the emancipator are the only ones to inherit because of it. Women do not inherit from patronage, except the property of slaves whom they have emancipated, or who have been emancipated by someone whom they have emancipated. The same applies to every quota-heir *[dhū farḍ]*, except the father and the grandfather, each of whom is entitled to one sixth, together with the son and his son, and the patronage belongs to the nearest in kin.

If the emancipator dies leaving two sons and his emancipated slave, and one of the two sons dies leaving a son, then his emancipated slave dies, his estate belongs to the son of the emancipator. If the two sons die after him and before the client, and one of them leaves a son and the other leaves nine, his patronage is shared among them in proportion to their number, so each of them is entitled to one tenth.

If a woman emancipates a male slave, then dies, his patronage belongs to her son, and his blood money is incumbent on her residuary heirs.

Chapter

Emancipation
[al-ʿItq]

Emancipation *[ʿitq]* is the liberation *[taḥrīr]* of a slave. It is brought about by word and deed.

As for emancipation by word, it results from the explicit use of the terms *ʿitq* and *taḥrīr* and their derivatives. When the owner makes such a statement, emancipation therefore comes about, even if he does not intend it. On the other hand, if he uses other terms that may implicitly suggest emancipation, his statement does not result in emancipation, unless that is what he intends.

As for emancipation by deed, when someone acquires the ownership of a *dhū raḥim marḥam* [a relative on the maternal side, in a degree of consanguinity precluding marriage], that slave is thereby emancipated. If someone emancipates part of a slave, either generally or specifically, the whole of him is emancipated. If he emancipates part of a slave whose ownership is shared, and he has the means to pay the price of his co-owner's share, the whole of the slave is emancipated. He is obliged to pay his co-owner for his share, and he is entitled to the patronage of the emancipated slave. If he lacks the means, however, he emancipates only his own share, because of the saying of Allāh's Messenger (Allāh bless him and give him peace):

> If someone emancipates a share of his in a slave, and he has enough to pay the price of the slave, he must assign a fair value to him and give his partners their shares. The slave will then be wholly emancipated. If he does not have enough, the slave will be emancipated to whatever extent he has been emancipated.

If someone acquires the ownership of part of a *dhū raḥim* of his, he is obliged to emancipate the remainder of that slave, if he has sufficient means, unless he acquires him by inheritance, in which case he is only obliged to emancipate the part that he has acquired.

Subsection

If someone says to his slave: "You are free," at a time that he names, or he makes his emancipation dependent on a precondition, the slave will be emancipated when that time comes, or when the precondition is fulfilled, and he will not be emancipated before that. The owner does not have the right to cancel the emancipation by word, but he is entitled to sell him, to present him as a gift, and to make use of him. When he returns to him, the precondition also returns. In the case of a slave woman who is pregnant at the time when the precondition is stipulated, or when it is fulfilled, the child in her womb is emancipated, but if she becomes pregnant and gives birth in the interval, her child is not emancipated.

Chapter

The Promise of Emancipation on the Owner's Death *[at-Tadbīr]*

If someone says to his slave: "You are free after my death," or words to that effect, he becomes a *mudabbar*, meaning a slave who will be emancipated on the death of his owner, if his value does not exceed the third [of the estate that may be bequeathed]. What exceeds [the bequeathable third] will not be emancipated, except with the permission of the heirs. The owner is entitled to sell him and present him as a gift, and to have sexual intercourse with a female slave. When he reacquires ownership of him, his promise of emancipation *[tadbīr]* returns.

If a slave woman bears children fathered by someone other than himself, her owner is entitled to take charge of them—whether she is a *mudabbara* [who has been promised emancipation on her owner's death], a *mukātaba* [holder of a written contract by which she becomes free on the payment of a certain sum], or an *umm walad* [mother of her owner's child].

It is permissible to promise *tadbīr* to the *mukātab*, and to make the contract of *kitāba* with the *mudabbar*.

Chapter

The Slave who Purchases his Emancipation *[al-Mukātab]*

The term *kitāba* signifies the written contract by which the slave buys himself from his owner, with money acquired for the purpose in accordance with the contract. If the slave who requests it of his owner is capable of earning by honest means, a positive response to his request is recommendable, because of the saying of Allāh (Exalted is He):

And those of your slaves who seek the written contract [of emancipation], contract with them accordingly, if you are aware of something good in them. (24:33)	*wa 'lladhīna yabtaghūna 'l-kitāba mimmā malakat aimānu-kum fa-kātibū-hum in ʿalimtum fī-him khairan.*

The payment should be made in installments, so the slave is emancipated when he has paid the full amount. He should also be given one quarter of the amount stipulated in his contract, because of the saying of Allāh (Exalted is He):

And give them some of the wealth of Allāh that He has given you.	*wa ātū-hum min māli 'llāhi 'lladhī ātā-kum.*

According to ʿAlī (may Allāh be well pleased with him), this means one quarter.

The *mukātab* continues to be a slave as long as he owes a single dirham [silver coin], except that he has the right to buy and sell, to travel, and to engage in whatever is of benefit to him financially. He is not entitled to make donations, nor to marry, nor to take a woman as a concubine, except with the permission of his owner. His owner is not entitled to employ him as a servant, or to take anything from his property. When he does take something from him, or commits a crime against him or against his property, he is subject to its penalty.

Interest *[ribā]* accrues between them in the same manner as between strangers, except that there is no objection to the slave's accelerating payment to his owner, and to the owner's exempting him from part of his contract *[kitāba]*.

The owner is not entitled to have sexual intercourse with his *mukātaba*, nor with her daughter, nor with her slave girl. If he does so, he is obliged to provide the bridal dower appropriate to a woman of her kind. If she bears him a child, she becomes an *umm walad*. If she fulfills her contract she is emancipated. She is also emancipated if her owner dies before she has fulfilled it, and whatever is in her possession belongs to her, unless she has failed to make the payment that was due [while he was still alive].

It is permissible to sell the *mukātab*, because ʿĀʾisha (may Allāh be well pleased with her) bought Buraira, who was a *mukātaba*, at the command of Allāh's Messenger (Allāh bless him and give him peace). When the *mukātab* is sold, he remains in the possession of his purchaser for the remainder of his contract *[kitāba]*. Then, if he fulfills it, he is emancipated and his patronage belongs to his purchaser, but if he is incapable of fulfilling it, he is a slave.

If each of two *mukātab*'s purchases the other, the purchase of the first is valid, and the purchase of the second is invalid. If the first of them does not know [that he is purchasing a *mukātab*], both sales are null and void.

If the *mukātab* dies, the contract *[kitāba]* is annulled. If the owner dies before him, he is obliged to fulfill his contract by making payment to the heirs.

The *kitāba* is a binding contract, which neither of the two parties is entitled to revoke. If an installment falls due, but the *mukātab* does not pay it on time, his owner is entitled to pester him.

If the slave and the owner disagree about the *kitāba*, or the *tadbīr*, or the *istīlād* [fathering of a slave woman's child], the word is the word of the owner, together with his oath.

Chapter

The Rules that apply to *Ummahāt al-Awlād* [Slave Women who become the Mothers of their Owners' Children]

If a slave woman becomes pregnant by her owner, and then delivers something that is clearly human in character, she thereby becomes related to him as an *umm walad* [mother of her owner's child]. She will be emancipated on his death, even if she is the only slave woman in his possession, but she is his slave as long as he is still alive. The rules that apply to her are the rules that apply to slave women in general, with regard to the lawfulness of sexual intercourse with her, the ownership of her benefits and her acquisitions, and all other rules, except that her owner does not have the right to sell her, nor to pawn her, nor to transfer ownership of her by any other means.

It is permissible for her to make and receive testamentary bequests.

If she kills her owner with deliberate intent, she is subject to retaliation. If she kills him by mistake, she is liable for her own price. She is emancipated in both cases.

If someone other than her owner has sexual intercourse with a slave woman in marriage, then acquires ownership of her while she is pregnant, the child in the womb is emancipated and he is entitled to sell her.

The Book of Marriage
[Kitāb an-Nikāḥ]

The Book of Marriage
[Kitāb an-Nikāḥ]

Marriage is one of the exemplary customs *[sunan]* of the Messengers. It is more meritorious than abstaining from it for the sake of supererogatory worship, because the Prophet (Allāh bless him and give him peace) refused to allow ʿUthmān ibn Maẓʿūn to practice such abstinence, and he said:

> O you young men, if any one of you is capable of providing, let him marry, for that is the best safeguard of modesty and chastity. If he cannot [afford to marry], he must fast, for that will be a form of castration for him.

If someone intends to a make a marriage proposal to a woman, he is entitled to view those parts of her body that are normally apparent, like her face, her palms and her feet. A man should not offer a proposal in competition with his brother's proposal, unless the latter is not accepted. It is not permissible to make an explicit proposal to a woman who is observing the *ʿidda* [period of waiting prescribed after widowhood or divorce]. In the special case of an irrevocably divorced woman, however, it is permissible to offer an implicit proposal, by saying: "Do not give me the slip, for I am very fond of someone like you," or words to that effect. Marriage is not contracted without consent from the woman's guardian or his deputy, who must say: "I have married you [to my ward]," and acceptance from the husband or his deputy, who must say: "I have accepted," or "I have become espoused."

Before the marriage is contracted, it is commendable to deliver the sermon of Ibn Masʿūd (may Allāh be well pleased with him), who said: "Allāh's Messenger (Allāh bless him and give him peace) taught us to declare on such occasions:

> Praise is due to Allāh. We praise Him, we appeal to Him for help, we seek His forgiveness and we repent to Him. We take refuge with Allāh from the vices of our lower selves and from the evils of our deeds. He whom Allāh

guides has no one to lead him astray, and he whom He causes to stray has no guide. I bear witness that there is no god but Allāh, and I bear witness that Muḥammad is His servant and His Messenger."

It is also appropriate to recite these three Qurʾānic verses:

O you who truly believe,	*yā ayyuha 'lladhīna*
observe your duty to Allāh,	*āmanu 'ttaqu 'llāha*
with the devotion that	*ḥaqqa tuqāti-hi*
is truly due to Him,	
and do not die except as	*wa lā tamūtunna illā*
those who have surrendered. (3:102)	*wa antum muslimīn.*
And be careful to observe	*wa 'ttaqu 'llāha 'lladhī*
your duty to Allāh,	
whom you invoke when making	*tasāʾalūna bi-hi*
claims of one another,	
and to the wombs	*wa 'l-arḥām:*
[that bore you].	
Allāh is always	*inna 'llāha kāna*
Watchful over you. (4:1)	*ʿalai-kum Raqībā.*
O you who truly believe,	*yā ayyuha 'lladhīna*
you must practice true	*āmanu 'ttaqu 'llāha*
devotion to Allāh,	
and use speech that gets	*wa qūlū qawlan sadīdā.*
straight to the point.	
He will improve your works	*yuṣliḥ la-kum aʿmāla-kum*
for you and He will forgive	*wa yaghfir la-kum*
you your sins.	*dhunūba-kum :*
Whoever obeys Allāh	*wa man yuṭiʿi 'llāha*
and His Messenger,	*wa Rasūla-hu*
he has truly won a	*fa-qad fāza*
mighty triumph. (33:70,71)	*fawzan ʿaẓīmā.*

It is also commendable to publicize the marriage, and for the women to celebrate it by beating on their tambourines.

Chapter

Marriage Guardianship
Walāyat am-Nikāḥ

There is no marriage without a guardian and two male witnesses from among the Muslims. For giving a free woman in marriage, the person best qualified is her father, then his father, and so on in the ascending line of generations, then her son, then his son, and so on in the descending line, then the closest of her paternal relatives, then her emancipator [if she has been freed from slavery], then the closest of his paternal relatives, then the ruler *[sulṭān]*. Each of these may be represented by his agent. When a closer relative exists, it is not permissible for a more distant relative to give in marriage, unless the former is a minor, or mentally incompetent, or a member of a different religion, or wrongfully opposed to the marriage, or absent in a remote location. No one has guardianship of a member of a different religion, except a Muslim if he is a ruler or the chieftain of a community.

Subsection

The father is entitled to give his minor children, male and female, and his virgin daughters, in marriage without their consent. In the case of the adult virgin, seeking her consent is recommended. As for his adult sons, and his widowed or divorced daughters, he is not entitled to give them in marriage without their consent. The other guardians are not entitled to give a minor male or female in marriage, nor to give an adult female in marriage without her consent. The consent of the widow or divorcée is expressed in speech, while the consent of the virgin is indicated by silence, because of the saying of

Allāh's Messenger (Allāh bless him and give him peace):

> The widow is more entitled to decide for herself than her guardian. The virgin should be asked to consent on her own behalf, and her consent is her silence.

A woman's guardian is not entitled to give her in marriage to anyone who is not a suitable match for her. The Arabs are suitable matches for one another. The slave is not a suitable match for a free woman, nor is the immoral sinner a suitable match for virtuous woman.

If someone wishes to marry a woman of whom he is the guardian, he is entitled to marry her on his own behalf with her consent. If he marries his female slave to his minor male slave, it is permissible for him to assume responsibility for both sides of the contract. If he says to his female slave, in the presence of two male witnesses: "I have emancipated you and made your emancipation your dower," both the emancipation and the marriage are established, because Allāh's Messenger (Allāh bless him and give him peace) emancipated Ṣafiyya and made her emancipation her dower.

Subsection

The master is entitled to give all his female slaves, and his minor male slaves, in marriage without their consent, but he does not have the right to compel his adult male slave to marry. Whenever a male slave marries without his master's consent, he is guilty of fornication. If he cohabits with the woman, he is responsible for her dower as well as his criminal offense, unless the master ransoms him with no less than his value or the dower. If someone marries a female slave on the assumption that she is free, then comes to know the truth, he is entitled to annul the marriage. No dower is required of him if he annuls before consummation, but if he cohabits with her she is entitled to her dower. If he makes her pregnant, her son will be free. He will ransom him with his value, and recover what he has lost from the person who deceived him. The couple will be separated, if he is not one of those who are permitted to marry female slaves, but if he is one of those for whom that is permissible, he will accept the marriage, and any child she produces after the acceptance will be a slave.

Chapter

Women with whom Marriage is Unlawful
Al-Muḥarramāt fi'-Nikāḥ

They are mothers, daughters and sisters, brothers' daughters and sisters' daughters, paternal aunts and maternal aunts, the mothers of wives, the wives of fathers and sons, and stepdaughters with whose mothers marriage has been consummated. Foster relationship makes marriage unlawful in the same way as kinship. The daughters of unlawful women are unlawful, except the daughters of paternal and maternal aunts, those of the mothers of wives, and those of the wives of fathers and sons. Their mothers are also unlawful, except those of the daughters, stepdaughters and wives of fathers and sons. If someone has sexual intercourse with a woman—lawful or unlawful—she is unlawful to his father and his son, and her mothers and daughters are unlawful to him.

Subsection

It is unlawful to be married to two sisters at the same time, and likewise to a woman and her paternal or maternal aunt, because of the saying of Allāh's Messenger (Allāh bless him and give him peace):

> You must not be married to a woman and her paternal aunt at the same time, nor to both her and her maternal aunt.

It is not permissible for a free man to have more than four wives at the same time, nor for a slave to have more than two. If someone combines those whom he is not permitted to combine in a single contract, the contract is invalid. If he does so in two contracts, the second of them is not valid.

If an unbeliever accepts Islām when he has two sisters at his disposal, he must choose one of the two. If they are a mother and daughter, and he has not cohabited with the mother, her marriage alone will be annulled. If he has cohabited with her, both of their marriages will be annulled, and both the mother and the daughter will become permanently unlawful to him. If he accepts Islām when he has more than four wives at his disposal, he must keep four of them and separate from the rest, regardless of whether he keeps the first or the last of those with whom he contracted marriage. The same applies in the case of a slave, if he accepts Islām when he has more than two women at his disposal. If someone divorces a wife and marries her sister, or her maternal aunt, or any fifth wife during the *ʿidda* [waiting period] of the divorcée, the marriage is not valid, regardless of whether the divorce is revocable or irrevocable.

Subsection

It is permissible for a man to own two sisters [as slaves], and he is entitled to have sexual intercourse with one of them. As soon as he does so, her sister becomes unlawful to him, until the one with whom he has cohabited becomes unlawful, through being given in marriage or removed from his ownership, and he knows that she is not pregnant. If he has intercourse with the second, and the first then returns to his ownership, she will not be lawful to him until the other becomes unlawful. The slave girl's paternal and maternal aunts are like her sister in this regard.

Subsection

The Muslim is not entitled, even if he is a slave, to marry an unbelieving slave girl. Nor is a free man entitled to marry a Muslim slave girl, unless he cannot find the means to support a free women, or the price of a slave girl, and he is afraid of committing fornication. He is entitled to marry four, provided that the necessary preconditions are fulfilled.

The Book of Foster Relationship *[Kitāb ar-Riḍā']*

The Book of Foster Relationship
[Kitāb ar-Riḍā‘]

The rules of foster relationship are the same as the rules of kinship, with regard to the prohibition of marriage and the state of consanguinity. When a woman breast-feeds a child, he therefore becomes a son to her, and also to the man whose sexual intercourse results in the milk she produces. It is thus unlawful for her foster son to marry any of those women who are unlawful to her son by kinship, because of the saying of Allāh's Messenger (Allāh bless him and give him peace):

> Unlawful because of foster relationship is whatever is unlawful because of kinship.

As for the marital unlawfulness due to fosterage, it is caused by the milk that is swallowed, whether it enters the throat by sucking from the breast, or by drinking or snuffing, and whether it is pure or mixed, so long as it has not been spoiled.

Foster milk does not cause marital unlawfulness except on three conditions:

1. It must be the milk of a woman, whether she is a virgin or a non-virgin, and whether it is drunk during her life or after her death. As for the milk of an animal, or a man, or a hermaphrodite, it does not make anything unlawful.
2. It must be drunk during the two years [of infancy], because of the saying of Allāh's Messenger (Allāh bless him and give him peace):

   > No kind of suckling causes marital unlawfulness, except that which opens the intestines and occurs before weaning.

3. The child must take five sucks, because of the saying of ‘Ā’isha: "It was revealed in the Qur’ān that ten sucks cause marital unlawfulness, but five of those were annulled, so it came to be that five known sucks cause marital unlawfulness. When Allāh's

Messenger died (Allāh bless him and give him peace), the matter was settled on that basis."

The milk [produced by the semen] of the polygamist causes marital unlawfulness. If a man has two wives, therefore, and one of them uses his milk to suckle a male child, while the other suckles a female child, the two children become brother and sister, because the semen [that produces the milk] is one and the same. If one of the two wives uses his milk to give three breast-feedings to a female child, then the other wife gives her two breast-feedings, she becomes a daughter to him, but not to them. If the girl became a wife of his, her marriage would be annulled and he would be liable for half of her dower, to be reclaimed from them in fifths, but their marriage to him would not be annulled. If one of his two wives gave the female child five breast-feedings, three from his milk and two from the milk of another man, she would become a mother to her and they would both be unlawful to him, while the girl would also be permanently unlawful to the other man. If the girl did not become a wife of his, the marriage of the foster mother would not be annulled. If a woman married a boy child, and gave him five breast-feedings, she would be unlawful to him and her marriage would be annulled. She would also be unlawful to the producer of the milk, on a permanent basis, because she had become one of the wives of his sons.

Subsection

If a man married an adult woman, but did not cohabit with her, and he also married a minor, whom the adult woman suckled, the adult woman would be unlawful to him, while the marriage of the minor would be established. If he married two minors, and the adult woman suckled them both, the adult woman would be unlawful to him, the marriage of the two minors would be annulled, and he would be entitled to marry whichever of the two minors he wished. If they were three, and she suckled each of them separately, the adult woman would be unlawful to him, the marriage of the first two to be suckled would be annulled, and the marriage of the third would be established. If she suckled one of them separately, and then two together, the marriage of all three would be annulled, and he would be entitled to contract a separate marriage with whichever of them he wished. If he had cohabited with the adult woman, all of the would be permanently unlawful to him. No dower would be due to the adult woman if he had not cohabited with her, but if he had done so she would be entitled to her dower. He would also be liable for half of the dower of the minors, to be reclaimed from the adult woman. If the minor crept in beside the adult woman, while she was asleep, and took five sucks from her, they would both be unlawful to the husband, and the adult would be entitled to half of her dower, to be reclaimed by him from the minor, if this took place before cohabitation. If it happened after that, she would be entitled to the whole of her dower, which he could not reclaim from anyone, and no dower would be due to the minor. If he married a woman, then said: "She is my sister by fosterage," her marriage would be annulled. She would be entitled to half of her dower if he had cohabited with her, and half of the dower if he had not cohabited with her, and if she did not believe him. If she believed him before cohabitation, she would not be entitled to anything. If it is she who says: "He is my brother by fosterage," but he calls her a liar and she has no proof, she is his wife according to the law.

Chapter

Marriage to the Unbelievers
Nikāḥ al Kuffār

It is not permissible for a Muslim woman to marry an unbeliever, under any circumstances, nor for a Muslim man to marry an unbeliever, except a free woman of scriptural religion. Whenever the husband of a woman of scriptural religion accepts Islām, or two unbelieving spouses accept Islām together, their marriage remains intact. If one of them accepts Islām, other than the husband of a woman of scriptural religion, or if one of two Muslim spouses apostasizes before consummation, the marriage is immediately annulled. If that happens after consummation, and the one who is an unbeliever accepts Islām during the woman's *ʿidda* [period of waiting], their marriage remains intact. They must otherwise face the fact that the marriage has been annulled from the moment when their religion differed. When something has been assigned to her [as a dower] while they were both unbelievers, and she has taken possession of it during their unbelief, nothing else is due to her, even if it is unlawful. If she has not taken possession of it, and it is unlawful, she is entitled to the dower of a woman like her, or half of it when that is appropriate.

Subsection

Suppose a free man accepts Islām when he has female slaves at his disposal, and they accept Islām together with him. If the state of their being together in Islām is such that he is someone for whom it is not permissible to marry female slaves, their marriage is annulled. If he is someone for whom it is permissible to marry them, he should keep as many of them as are suitable for him, and separate from the rest.

Chapter

Stipulations attached to Marriage
Ash-Shurūṭ fi 'n-Nikāḥ

If the woman stipulates her home or her town, or that the husband will not marry another wife, or that he will not take a slave girl as a concubine, she is entitled to her stipulation. If he does not fulfill it for her, the marriage will be annulled, because of the saying of Allāh's Messenger (Allāh bless him and give him peace):

> Of all stipulations, those most deserving of your fulfillment are those by which you make the private parts of women lawful to you.

Allāh's Messenger (Allāh bless him and give him peace) also forbade the marriage known as *mut'a*, by which he marries her for a specified period of time. It is likewise invalid for him to stipulate that he will divorce her at a particular time. He also forbade the practice known as *shighār*, by which one man gives his daughter in marriage to another, on condition that the other gives his daughter in marriage to him, and neither of them provides a dower. Allāh's Messenger (Allāh bless him and give him peace) also cursed those who engage in the practice by which a man marries a woman who has been repudiated three times, [with the intention of divorcing her] in order to make her lawful to the man who repudiated her.

Chapter

Defects for which Marriage may be Annulled
Al-ʿUyūb allatī yufsakh bi-ha 'n-Nikāḥ

Whenever one of the two spouses discovers that the other is a slave, or a lunatic, or a leper, or a victim of elephantiasis, or the man discovers that the woman is one whose vagina is completely closed up, or she discovers that he has had his penis cut off, the offended party is entitled to have the marriage annulled, provided that he or she had no knowledge of that before the contract, but the annulment is not permissible except by the verdict of a judge. Suppose the woman claims that her husband is impotent, so he does not have sexual intercourse with her, and he admits that he has not had intercourse with her for the period of a year since his arraignment on this charge. If he still does not have sexual intercourse with her, she then has the choice of staying with him or separating from him. If she chooses to separate from him, the judge will formally separate them, unless she knew about his impotence before her marriage, or unless she said at any time: "I am satisified with him as an impotent." If she came to know of his impotence after the contract, but refrained from expressing an appeal, her right is not forfeited. Suppose he says: "She came to know of my impotence, but she was satisfied with me after coming to know." If she contradicts him, her statement is the one accepted. If he has had sexual intercourse with her on one occasion, he is not impotent. If he makes that claim, but she contradicts him, then, if she was a virgin [when she married him], trustworthy women should be consulted and their opinion respected. If she was a widow or divorcée, the last word is his statement together with his oath.

Subsection

If the woman is emancipated while her husband is a slave, she is given the choice between staying with him or separating from him, and she is entitled to separate from him without the verdict of a judge. If he is emancipated before she makes her choice, or if he has sexual intercourse with her, her freedom of choice is annulled. If she is only partially emancipated, or emancipated completely while her husband is a free man, she has no freedom of choice.

The Book of the Bridal Dower

[Kitāb aṣ-Ṣadāq]

The Book of the Bridal Dower
[Kitāb aṣ-Ṣadāq]

Everything that is permissible as a price is also permissible as a bridal dower *[ṣadāq]*, whether it be little or much, because of the response of Allāh's Messenger (Allāh bless him and give him peace) to someone who said to him: "Give me this woman in marriage, if you have no need of her." He said:

> Provide some token, if only a ring of iron!

If a man gives his daughter in marriage for any bridal dower, it is therefore permissible. No one other than the father may deprive her of the dower that is usually given to her equal, except with her consent. If he specifies a particular slave as the dower, and she finds him defective, she may choose between accepting compensation for his defect and rejecting him, or receiving his price. If she finds him to be wrongfully appropriated, or emancipated, she is entitled to his price. If she is aware of his freedom or his misappropriation at the time of the contract, she is entitled to the dower of her equal. If the husband marries her on condition that he will purchase a particular slave for her, but his master does not sell him, or demands a higher price than he is worth, she is entitled to his normal price.

Subsection

If the husband marries her without a bridal dower, the marriage is valid. If he divorces her by repudiation before consummation, she is not entitled to anything except the *mut'a* [compensation paid to a divorced woman], in proportion to the ability of the wealthy and the ability of the needy. The maximum is a manservant, and the minimum is an article of clothing in which it is permissible for her to perform the ritual prayer.

If one of the two parties dies before the marriage is consummated and the dower is allotted, she is entitled to the usual dower of women like herself, no less and no more. The one who survives is entitled to the inheritance, and if it is the woman, she is obliged to observe the *ʿidda* [prescribed period of waiting before remarriage], because of the following precedent: In the case of Burūʿ bint Wāhiq, when her husband died without having consummated the marriage, and without having allotted her dower, the Prophet (Allāh bless him and give him peace) decreed that she was entitled to the usual dower of women like herself, no less and no more, that she was entitled to the inheritance, and that the *ʿidda* was incumbent upon her.

If she demands of him, before the consummation, that he allot her dower to her, she is entitled to that. If he allots her the usual dower of women like herself, or more, she is not entitled to anything else. The same rule applies if he allots her less than that, and she consents.

Subsection

Her dower is canceled by any cause of separation that comes from the woman, such as her embracing Islām, or her apostasy, or her fosterage, or annulment due to his deficiency or his insolvency, or her emancipation from slavery. If it comes from the husband, such as his divorcing her by repudiation *[ṭalāq]* and his divorcing her by *khulʿ* [at her request and on receipt of compensation from her], her dower is halved between them, unless he exempts her from his half, or she exempts him from her rightful share, assuming that she is mature, in which case the whole of the dower belongs to the other party. If it comes from a stranger, half of the dower is incumbent on the husband, who may claim its restitution from the person who has separated them.

When the dower is to be divided between the two parties, and it consists of something permanent, the value of which has not changed, it is divided between them in two equal halves. If it has been increased by a separate addition, like sheep that have given birth to lambs, the increase belongs to her, and the sheep are divided between them. If it has been increased by an inseparable addition, as when the sheep have grown fat, the woman is free to choose between receiving half of them in their increased condition, and receiving half of their value on the day of the marriage contract. If they have diminished, she is entitled to half of their value on the day of the marriage contract. If they have been damaged, she is entitled to half of their value on the day of the marriage contract.

When the husband has had sexual intercourse with her, the dower is established and it is not annulled by anything. If he has been with her in private after the contract, but he says: "I have not had intercourse with her," and she confirms his statement, the dower is established and the *ʿidda* must be observed.

If the two spouses disagree about the dower or its amount, the word is the word of the one who claims the usual dower, together with his or her oath.

Chapter

The Proper Treatment of Women *[Mu'āsharat an-Nisā']*

It is incumbent on the two spouses to treat each other with fair and friendly kindness, and to fulfill each other's rightful due without delay and without begrudging the effort. The husband's rightful claim on his wife is her submission and obedience to him in lovemaking, whenever he wishes, so long as she has no valid excuse. If she does that, she is entitled to have him satisfy all her needs for living expenses, clothing, and accommodation, by providing what is normal for wives like herself. If he withholds that from her, or part of it, but she can count on him to provide some means of support, she should get enough from him to look after herself and her children with proper care, because it is related that, when Hind told the Prophet (Allāh bless him and give him peace): "Abū Sufyān is a niggardly man, and he does not give me enough income to take care of myself and my children," he said to her:

> You must get enough to look after yourself and your children with proper care.

If she cannot get enough, because of his impoverishment or his withholding, so she opts for separation from him, the judge will separate them, whether the husband is a minor or an adult.

If she is a minor, with whom sexual enjoyment is impossible, or she does not submit to him, or she does not pay him the obedience he is entitled to receive from her, or she travels on her own business, without his permission or with his permission, he is not obliged to provide her with means of support.

Subsection

The husband is obliged to spend one night out of every four in her company, if she is a free woman, and one out every eight if she is a slave, unless he has a valid excuse. He is also obliged to copulate with her once in every four months, unless he has a valid excuse. If he swears to abstain from conjugal intercourse with her for more than four months, so she waits for four months and then brings him before the judge, but he denies the oath of abstinence or the expiration of the four months, or he claims that he copulated with her, and she is a non-virgin, the word is his word together with his oath. If he acknowledges that [oath of abstinence], he will be ordered to expiate it on her demand, and that means engaging in conjugal intercourse. If he expiates, Allāh is All-Forgiving, All-Compassionate, but if he does not expiate, he will be ordered to divorce her by repudiation *[ṭalāq]*. If he does divorce her by repudiation, the matter is settled, but if not, the judge will issue a decree of divorce against him. Then, if he returns to her, or leaves her until she is separated by the divorce and then remarries her, when he has kept the oath for more than the period of four months, his obligation to her is as I have described. If someone is incapable of expiation on her demand, he must say: "When I am able, I shall have conjugal intercourse with her," and postpone the expiation until he is capable of it.

Chapter

The Apportionment [of the husband's company among his wives] and the Violation of Marital Duties *[al-Qasm wa 'n-Nushūz]*

The man is obliged to treat his women equitably in the apportionment [of his company] and his support during the night. He must allot one night to the slave woman, and two nights to the free woman, even if she is a *Kitābiyya* [member of a Scriptural religion]. Where sexual intercourse is concerned, however, he is not obliged to treat them equally. He is not entitled to give precedence to one of them in the apportionment, nor in traveling with her, except by casting lots, for the Prophet (Allāh bless him and give him peace) once said:

> If he intends to make a journey, he must cast lots among his women, and the one who leaves with him will be the one whose arrow is cast.

The woman is entitled to give her rightful share in the apportionment to one of her co-wives, with her husband's consent. Alternatively, she may give it to him, so he may assign it whichever of them he wishes, because Sawda gave her day to ʿĀʾisha, so Allāh's Messenger (Allāh bless him and give him peace) allotted both her own day and Sawda's day to ʿĀʾisha.

When he becomes the bridegroom of a virgin, he should spend seven nights with her, then take turns. If he becomes the bridegroom of a non-virgin, he should spend three nights with her, because of the saying of Anas: "According to the Sunna, if he marries a virgin in addition to a non-virgin, he should spend seven nights with her. If he marries a non-virgin in addition to a virgin, he should spend three nights with her." If the non-virgin would like him to spend seven nights with her, he may do so and allot them to the others as well, because the Prophet (Allāh bless him and give him peace), when he married Umm Salama, spent three nights with her, then said:

> If you wish, I shall spend three nights with you, exclusively devoted to you, and if you wish, I shall allot seven to you. If I do allot seven to you, I shall allot seven to all my women.

Subsection

Strict privacy is recommended at the time of conjugal intercourse, and the husband should repeat the saying reported by Ibn ʿAbbās:

> If one of you says, when he comes to his wife: "In the Name of Allāh. O Allāh, keep Satan away from us, and keep Satan away from what You have provided for us," then, if a child is conceived between them, Satan will never harm the child.

Subsection

If the woman is afraid that her husband may violate her rights or reject her, nothing wrong is done if she seeks to please him by forfeiting some of her rights, as Sawda did when she was afraid that Allāh's Messenger (Allāh bless him and give him peace) might divorce her by repudiation.

If the man is afraid that his wife may violate his rights, he should caution her. Then, if she displays a violation, he should avoid contact with her in bed. If that does not deter her, he is entitled to beat her without inflicting severe pain.

If the discord between them is considered dangerous, the judge must send an arbitrator from his family and an arbitrator from her family, both of them believers, who will reconcile them if they see fit, or separate them. Whatever the arbitrators do in that regard, it is binding on the two spouses.

Chapter

Divorce at the Instance of the Wife *[al-Khulʿ]*

If the woman is filled with hatred for the man, and she is afraid that she may not observe the legal rules of Allāh in her obedience to him, she is entitled to ransom herself from him, for whatever compensation is agreed between them. In accordance with recommended practice, he should not take from her more than [the bridal dower] he gave her. If he divorces her by *khulʿ* [at her instance] or by repudiation *[ṭalāq]* in exchange for compensation, she is separated from him and his repudiation has no effect on her after that, even if he confronts her with it.

Divorce by *khulʿ* is permissible in exchange for anything that is permissible as a bridal dower, and also for an unknown amount of compensation. If she says: "Divorce me by *khulʿ* in exchange for the dirhams [silver coins] in my hand," or, "whatever valuable property is in my home," and he does so, the divorce is valid, and he is entitled to what is in her hand or her home. If there is nothing in them, he is entitled to three dirhams or the least of what is called valuable property. If he divorces her by *khulʿ* in exchange for a particular slave, and he turns out to be defective, he is entitled to receive compensation for his defect, or to reject him and receive his price. If he turns out to be a misappropriated slave, or a free man, he is entitled to his price [as a legitimate slave].

Divorce by *khulʿ* is permissible for any man whose divorce by repudiation is permissible. Waiver of the compensation is not valid, except on the part of someone whose free disposal of property is valid.

The Book of Divorce by Repudiation
[Kitāb aṭ-Ṭalāq]

The Book of Divorce by Repudiation
[Kitāb aṭ-Ṭalāq]

Divorce by repudiation *[ṭalāq]* is not valid except from a husband who is a responsible adult and acting voluntarily. Divorce by repudiation is not valid if the husband is acting under coercion, or if he is not of sound mind, with the exception of the drunkard. The free man has the right to pronounce three repudiations [before the marriage is finally dissolved], whereas the slave may pronounce only two, whether the wife concerned is a free woman or a slave. When he has exhausted the number of his repudiations, the divorcée is not lawful to him until she has contracted a valid marriage with a different husband, and he has copulated with her, because Allāh's Messenger (Allāh bless him and give him peace) said to the divorced wife of Rifā'a:

> Perhaps you wish to return to Rifā'a? Not until you taste the honey [of another husband], and he tastes your honey!

It is not lawful to combine the three, nor to repudiate the wife during her menstruation, if he has already consummated their marriage, or during an inter menstrual period of purity in which he has had sexual intercourse with her. This rule is based on the following traditional report: 'Umar's son repudiated a wife of his while she was menstruating, so 'Umar mentioned that to Allāh's Messenger (Allāh bless him and give him peace) and he said:

> Command him to take her back, then keep her until she is ritually pure, then menstruates, then becomes ritually pure. If he still sees fit to repudiate her, let him repudiate her before he touches her.

As defined by the Sunna, divorce by repudiation is performed as follows: The husband repudiates his wife during an inter menstrual period of purity, in which he has not once had sexual intercourse with her, then he leaves her untouched until her *'idda* [prescribed period of waiting] is completed. In other words, whenever he says to her:

"You are repudiated in accordance with the Sunna," while she is in a period of ritual purity during which he has not had sexual intercourse with her, she is divorced by repudiation. On the other hand, if she is in a period of ritual purity during which he has had sexual intercourse with her, or in a period of menstruation, she may not be divorced by repudiation until she is pure and free from menstruation. If he says to her: "You are repudiated in accordance with the doctrine of innovation *[bidʿa]*," while she is menstruating, or in a period of ritual purity during which he has had sexual intercourse with her, she is divorced by repudiation. If she is not in the latter condition, she may not be divorced by repudiation until he has sexual intercourse with her, or she menstruates.

As for the wife whose marriage has not been consummated, the pregnant wife whose pregnancy is obvious, and the wife who is too old to menstruate, there is no restriction on her repudiation, neither in the Sunna nor in any doctrine of innovation. When he says to her: "You are repudiated in accordance with the Sunna, or in accordance with the doctrine of innovation," she is therefore immediately divorced by repudiation.

Chapter

Explicit Repudiation *[Ṣarīḥ aṭ-Ṭalāq]* and its Indirect Expression *[Kināya]*

Its explicit form is the use of the noun "*ṭalāq*" and its adjectival and verbal derivatives, as in the husband's saying: "You are repudiated *[ṭāliq* or *muṭallaqa]*," and, "I have repudiated you *[ṭallaqtu-ki]*." Whenever he pronounces the repudiation in such explicit terms, she is divorced by repudiation, even if that is not his intention. If someone asks him: "Do you have a wife?" and he says "No," with the intention of telling a lie, she is not divorced by repudiation, but if he says: "I have repudiated her *[ṭallaqtu-hā]*," she is divorced by repudiation, even if he intends to tell a lie. If he says to his wife: "You are free," or "separated," or "cut off," or "unmarried," intending to repudiate her thereby, she is divorced by threefold repudiation, unless he intends less than that. Any other indirect expression results in a single repudiation, unless he intends it to mean three.

If he gives his wife the option, and she prefers to go her own way, she is repudiated once, but if she prefers to stay with her husband, nothing happens. ʿĀʾisha said: "Allāh's Messenger (Allāh bless him and give him peace) gave us the option, so was it a repudiation?" The wife may not choose except on the occasion [when he gives her the option], unless he leaves her to decide at a later stage. If he says: "Your affair is in your own hand," or "repudiate me yourself," it is in her own hand, unless he revokes the option or has sexual intercourse with her.

Chapter

Making Repudiation Dependent on a Precondition *[Taʿlīq aṭ-Ṭalāq bi 'sh-Sharṭ]*

It is permissible to make the repudiation [of a wife] and the emancipation [of a slave woman] dependent on a precondition, after the marriage and the acquisition of ownership, but it is not valid beforehand. Were he to say: "If I marry so-and-so, she will be divorced by repudiation," or: "If I acquire ownership of her, she will be a free woman," neither the repudiation nor the emancipation would take effect.

[In Arabic] the appropriate conditional particles are six: (1) *in* [if], (2) *idhā* [if; when; as soon as; provided that], (3) *ayy* [whichever, whoever], (4) *matā* [when] (5) *man* [whoever] and (6) *kulla-mā* [whenever; every time that]. None of these implies the need for repetition, except *kulla-mā*, and once they are substantiated, their consequence is established. Thus, when he says: "If you stand up, you are divorced by repudiation," and she stands up, she is repudiated and the precondition is fulfilled. If he says: "Whenever you stand up, you are divorced by repudiation," she is repudiated each time she stands up. If the conditional phrase is negative, as in his saying: "If *[in]* I do not repudiate you, you are divorced by repudiation," and he does not repudiate her, she is kept in suspense; since he did not fix a specific time [for the repudiation to take effect], the divorce will only occur at the last of the possible times.

The other conditional particles imply immediacy, so if he says: "When *[matā]* I do not repudiate you, you are divorced by repudiation," and he does not repudiate her, she is divorced immediately. If he says:

"Whenever *[kulla-mā]* I do not repudiate you, you are divorced by repudiation," and enough time passes for him to be able to repudiate her thrice, but he does not repudiate her, she is divorced three times, if she is a wife whose marriage has been consummated. If he says: "Whenever *[kulla-mā]* you give birth to a child, you are divorced by repudiation," and she gives birth to twins, she is repudiated on the delivery of the first, and separated on the delivery of the second, because it marks the expiration of her *ʿidda* [period of waiting before the divorce becomes final], and she is not repudiated because of it.

If he says: "If you menstruate, you are divorced by repudiation," she is repudiated at the beginning of the menstrual period. If it becomes quite clear that it is not a menstrual period, she is not repudiated. If she says: "I have menstruated," but he calls her a liar, she is repudiated. If he says: "You have menstruated," but she calls him a liar, she is repudiated on the strength of his assertion. If he says: "If you menstruate, you and your co-wife are both divorced by repudiation," and if she then says: "I have menstruated," but he calls her a liar, she is repudiated but not her co-wife.

Chapter

How the Number of Repudiations Varies

If the wife is one whose marriage has not been consummated, her divorce is a single repudiation *[ṭalqa]*.

Reunion is made unlawful by three repudiations pronounced by the free man, and two pronounced by the slave, if they are inseparably combined, as in his saying: "You are divorced by threefold repudiation," or: "You are divorced by repudiation, divorced by repudiation, divorced by repudiation." They count as a single repudiation only, however, if he arranges them in sequence, by using expressions like: "You are divorced by repudiation, *and so* divorced by repudiation," or: "You are divorced by repudiation, *then* divorced by repudiation," or: "You are divorced by repudiation, *or rather* divorced by repudiation," or: "If I repudiate you, you will be divorced by repudiation" (and he then repudiates her), or: "Whenever I do not repudiate you, you are divorced by repudiation."

If the wife is one whose marriage has been consummated, she is subject to every repudiation pronounced by the husband.

If someone is doubtful about the repudiation, or its number, or the foster relationship, or its reckoning, his decision should be based on what is known for certain.

If he says to his wives: "One of you is divorced by repudiation," without intending one of them in particular, the selection is made by casting lots.

If he repudiates a part of his wife's body, either collectively or specifically, like her finger or her hand, the whole of her is divorced by repudiation. This does not apply to the fingernail, the tooth, the hair, the saliva, the tears, and suchlike, so she is not divorced by their repudiation.

If he says: "You are divorced by half of a repudiation, or less than this," she is divorced by one complete repudiation.

Chapter

Restoration of the Marriage
[Raj'a or Rij'a]

If he repudiates his wife after consummation, without receiving compensation, fewer than three times, or fewer than two if he is a slave, he is entitled to restore their marriage, so long as she is still in the *'idda* [period of waiting]. This rule is based on the saying of Allāh (Exalted is He):

And their husbands would do better to take them back in that case, if they desire a reconciliation. (2:228)	*wa bu'ūlatu-hunna aḥaqqu bi-raddi-hinna fī dhālika in arādū iṣlāḥā.*

Restoration of the marriage is brought about by his saying to two men among the Muslims: "I testify that I have returned to my wife, or taken her back, or kept her," without involving a marriage guardian, without an extra bridal dower, and without her agreement. If he has sexual intercourse with her, it counts as a restoration.

The *raj'iyya* (or *rij'iyya*) is a wife who is subjected to repudiation *[ṭalāq]* or *ẓihār*,[18] but whose marriage may still be restored. She is entitled to beautify herself for her husband and treat him with respect, and he is entitled to have sexual intercourse with her, to be with her in private, and to travel with her. If he takes her back, she returns with the remainder of her [potential] repudiation still at his disposal. If he abandons her until she is divorced, then she marries another husband, from whom she is then divorced, and the first husband remarries her, she returns to him with the remainder of her [potential] repudiation still at his disposal. If they disagree about the completion

[18] See p. 243 below.

of her *ʿidda* [period of waiting before remarriage], the word is her word together with her oath, provided that what she claims on that score is possible. If the husband claims, after the completion of her *ʿidda*, that he had taken her back during her *ʿidda*, but she denies his claim, the word is her word. If he has proof, however, judgment will be given in his favor on the strength thereof. If she has already married another husband, she will therefore be returned to the first, whether or not the second has consummated their marriage.

Chapter

The *'Idda* [Period of Waiting after Widowhood or Repudiation]

No *'idda* is incumbent on a woman whose husband separates from her during his lifetime, before making physical contact and being with her in private seclusion, because of the saying of Allāh (Exalted is He):

O you who truly believe,	*yā ayyuha 'lladhīna āmanū idhā*
if you marry believing women,	*nakaḥtumu 'l-mu'mināti*
then divorce them before	*thumma ṭallaqtumū-hunna*
you have touched them,	*min qabli an tamassū-hunna*
there is then no period	*fa-mā la-kum 'alai-hinna min*
that you should reckon. (33:49)	*'iddatin ta'taddūna-hā.*

Those women who must observe the *'idda* are subdivided into four categories:

1. Those who are pregnant. Their *'idda* lasts until they deliver the children in their wombs. If a woman is pregnant with twins, her *'idda* does not expire until she delivers the second of them. As for the content of the womb that necessitates the *'idda*, and by which the slave woman acquires the status of an *umm walad* [mother of (her master's) child], it is that in which the nature of the human being is apparent.
2. Those who are widowed by the husband's death. They must wait by themselves for four months and ten days. In the case of slave women, the period is half of that. Whether the husband's death occurs before physical contact or after it, the same rule applies.
3. Women divorced by repudiation while they still experience menstrual periods. They must wait by themselves for three menstrual periods. In the case of the slave woman, the period of waiting is two menstruations.

4. Those who are beyond the age of menstruation, and those who have never menstruated. Their ʿ*idda* is three months. In the case of the slave woman, it is two months.

In accordance with Islāmic law, a period of waiting additional to the ʿ*idda* must be observed in three situations:

1. When the woman's menstruation ceases to occur, and she has no idea what has caused its cessation, she must wait for nine months, and then observe the ʿ*idda* of those beyond the age of menstruation. If she does know what has put a stop to her menstruation, she must remain in a state of ʿ*idda* until the menstruation resumes, and then observe the ʿ*idda* accordingly.
2. If the husband is missing, lost in a dangerous area, or completely out of touch with his family, so that no one has any news of him, his wife must wait for four years, and then observe the ʿ*idda* prescribed for widowhood. If he is missing in some other kind of situation, like the traveler engaged in trade, for instance, she may not remarry until she is absolutely certain of his death.
3. If the wife is doubtful after the expiration of her ʿ*idda*, because of the appearance of the signs of pregnancy, she may not remarry until the doubt has been cleared away. If she does remarry, the marriage is therefore invalid. If she is doubtful after her remarriage, it is not annulled unless she knew that she remarried while she was pregnant. When the woman observing the ʿ*idda* remarries, her remarriage is null and void, and the judge must separate the couple. If he separates them before consummation, she must complete the ʿ*idda* of the first husband. If the separation comes after consummation, she must complete the ʿ*idda* of the first from the time when the second cohabited with her, and then embark on the ʿ*idda* of the second. The second husband is then entitled to marry her after the expiration of the two ʿ*idda*'s. If she gives birth to a child from one of the two, his ʿ*idda* is thereby terminated, and she must observe the ʿ*idda* of the second. If it is possible for it to be from either of them, the judge must consult the physiognomists, and then assign it to whichever of them they assign it to. Her ʿ*idda* for him is thereby terminated, and she must observe the ʿ*idda* of the other.

Chapter

The Proper Observance of Mourning *[Iḥdād]*

The proper observance of mourning is incumbent on the woman whose husband has died. It consists of abstinence from finery, perfume, and kohl applied to the eyelids, as well as from wearing garments that are dyed to create a beautiful impression. This is based on the saying of Allāh's Messenger (Allāh bless him and give him peace):

> A woman must not mourn over a dead man for more than three [months], except over a husband, in which case she must mourn for four months and ten days.

She must not wear a garment that is dyed, with the exception of a garment made of cloth that is dyed before being woven. She must not use kohl and touch perfume, except a small amount of the aromatics called *qust* and *aẓfār*, which she may apply when she performs the major ablution. She must continue to reside in the house in which she was dwelling when the *ʿidda* became incumbent upon her, provided that is possible for her. If her husband dies when she has left home on a journey or a Pilgrimage, and she is still nearby, she must return to observe the *ʿidda* in her own home, but if she very far away, she must continue her journey.

The woman divorced by three repudiations is subject to the same rules as the widow, with the exception of observing the *ʿidda* in her own home.

Chapter

The Maintenance of Women Observing the ʿ*Idda* *[Nafaqat al-Muʿtaddāt]*

Such women fall into three categories:

1. The wife who has been repudiated, but whose marriage may still be restored. She is entitled to have maintenance and accommodation provided by her husband. If the husband of an unbelieving woman embraces Islām, or the wife of a Muslim apostatizes, neither woman is entitled to maintenance. If the wife of an unbeliever embraces Islām, or the husband of a Muslim apostatizes, after consummation, both women are entitled to maintenance during the ʿ*idda*.
2. The wife who is irrevocably divorced by repudiation or annulment while the husband is alive. She is not entitled to accommodation, whatever her condition may be. She is entitled to maintenance if she is pregnant, but otherwise not.
3. The wife who is widowed by her husband's death. She is not entitled to maintenance, nor to accommodation.

Chapter

Establishing the Marriageable Status of Slave Women *[Istibrāʾ al-Imāʾ]*

This is obligatory in three situations:

1. When someone acquires the ownership of a slave woman, he must abstain from sexual intercourse with her until he has established that she is not pregnant from her previous owner.
2. In the case of the *umm walad* [mother of (her master's) child], and the slave woman whose master has had sexual intercourse with her, it is not permissible for him to give her in marriage [to another man] until he has established that she is not pregnant, by abstaining from cohabiting with her.
3. If their master emancipates them [the *umm walad* or the slave woman with who he has had sexual intercourse], or they are emancipated by his death, they may not marry until they have personally established their freedom from pregnancy. That is established by the delivery of the child in the womb, if she is pregnant; or by menstruation if she experiences menstruation; or by the passage of a month if she is beyond the age of menstruation, or one of those who have never menstruated; or by the passage of ten months if her menstruation has ceased and she has no idea what caused its cessation.

The Book of Divorce by *Ẓihār*

The Book of Divorce by *Ẓihār*

Divorce by *ẓihār* is performed when the husband says to his wife: "You are like the back *[ẓahr]* of my mother," or he compares her to the back of any woman who is permanently unlawful to him, or he says: "You are like my father," with the intention of making her unlawful. She is not lawful to him after that, until he atones by emancipating a slave, before they touch each other. If he cannot find the means to emancipate a slave, he must fast for two consecutive months. If he cannot do that, he must feed sixty paupers. Such atonement is governed by the same rule, and has the same character, as the expiation of sexual intercourse during the month of Ramaḍān. If he copulates before the atonement, he is therefore guilty of sinful disobedience, and that same expiation is incumbent upon him.

If someone pronounces *ẓihār* against his wife several times, and does not atone, a single expiation is required. If he pronounces *ẓihār* against all his wives in a single sentence, a single expiation is likewise required, but if he pronounces it against them in several sentences, expiation for each one is incumbent upon him.

If he pronounces *ẓihār* against his slave woman, or declares her unlawful, or declares something permissible to be unlawful, or if the wife pronounces *ẓihār* against her husband, or declares him unlawful, the declaration does not result in unlawfulness, and its atonement is the expiation of an oath. The slave and the free man are alike in the matter of atonement, except that the slave does not atone except by fasting.

The Book
of Divorce by Mutual Cursing
[Kitāb al-Liʿān]

The Book of Divorce by Mutual Cursing *[Kitāb al-Liʿān]*

If the man slanderously accuses his wife of adultery, when she is an adult of sane mind, a free woman, chaste, and a Muslim, he is subject to the legal penalty *[ḥadd]*, if he does not swear the oath of mutual cursing. If she is a *dhimmiyya* [non-Muslim woman protected by Islāmic law],[19] or a slave woman, he is subject to censure, if he does not swear the oath of mutual cursing, but censure is not imposed on him until she demands it.

The oath of mutual cursing *[liʿān]* is sworn when the husband says, while pointing at his wife in the presence of the judge or his deputy: "I testify, by Allāh, that I am one of the truthful concerning the adultery that this wife of mine has committed." If she is not present, he must name her and her lineage. After swearing four times, he must be made to pause before the fifth, and he must be told: "Beware of offending Allāh, for this is binding, and the punishment of this world is far less serious than the punishment of the Hereafter!" If he still refuses to do anything other than complete his oath, he must say: "May the curse of Allāh be upon me, if I am one of the liars concerning the adultery that this wife of mine has committed."

The punishment is averted from the wife, if she then says four times: "I testify that he is one of the liars concerning the adultery of which he has accused me." She must then be made to pause before the fifth, and she must be filled with fear, as the man was filled with fear. If she still refuses to do anything other than complete her oath, she must say: "May the wrath of Allāh be upon me, if he is one of the truthful concerning the adultery of which this husband of mine has accused

[19] See note 21 on p. 279

me." The judge will then say: "I have separated the pair of you," and she will thus be rendered permanently unlawful to him.

If there is a child between them, but he disavows it, his paternity is negated—whether the child is still in the womb or has already been delivered—so long as he has not acknowledged it explicitly, or shown some sign from which acknowledgment can be inferred. This rule is based on the case reported by Ibn ʿUmar, in which a man repudiated his wife by *liʿān* and disavowed his paternity of her child, so Allāh's Messenger (Allāh bless him and give him peace) declared a permanent separation between them, and assigned the child to the mother.

Subsection

If a man's wife or his slave woman, with whom he has acknowledged having sexual intercourse, gives birth to a child, and he could possibly be its father, his paternity will be attached to it, because of the saying of Allāh's Messenger (Allāh bless him and give him peace):

> The child is for the [master of the] bed, and for the adulterer or fornicator there is stoning.

The wife's child is not disavowed except by *liʿān*, nor the child of the slave woman except by claiming the absence of her *istibrāʾ* [establishment of her marriageable status].[20] If he cannot possibly be the father, as when his slave woman gives birth within less than six months from his copulating with her, or his wife gives birth when less than that time has elapsed since their cohabitation was possible, or if the husband is the kind of man who does not father children—such as one who is under ten years of age, or a castrated eunuch—the child is not attributed to him.

Subsection

If two men have sexual intercourse with a woman during a single period of inter menstrual purity, because of mistaken identity, or if two co-owners have sexual intercourse with their slave woman during

[20] See p. 240 above.

a single period of inter menstrual purity, and she produces a child, or if two men claim the paternity of a child whose paternity is unknown, the physiognomists must examine its resemblance to them or their relatives, and the child will then be assigned to whichever of them they attribute it. If they attribute the child to them both, its paternity will be assigned to them both. If the problem is hard to resolve, or the physiognomists disagree, or no physiognomists can be found, the decision must be left until the child reaches puberty. The word of the physiognomist will not be accepted unless he is a fair and honest person, whose skill has passed the test of experience.

Chapter

Tutelage
[Ḥiḍāna]

The people most entitled to be in charge of the child's upbringing are the following, in order of priority: (1) its mother and then her mother and grandmothers of any generation; (2) the father and then his mother and grandmothers; (3) the grandfather and then his mother and grandmothers; (4) the full sister; (5) the sister on the father's side; (6) the sister on the mother's side; (7) the maternal aunt; (8) the paternal aunt; (9) other women relatives, in order of closeness; (10) other paternal relatives, in order of closeness.

No right of tutelage *[ḥiḍāna]* belongs to a slave, nor to an immoral profligate, nor to a woman married to a man who is unrelated to the child. If the obstacles are removed from them, however, they recover their right to tutelage.

When a boy reaches the age of seven, he is given the freedom to choose between his parents, so he then comes to be in the care of whichever of the two he selects. When a girl reaches the age of seven, her father is more entitled to her.

It is incumbent on the father to provide a wet nurse for his child, unless the mother wishes to suckle the child herself, for the remuneration appropriate to someone like her, since she is more entitled to the child than any other, whether she is married to the husband or divorced. If he has no father and no property, his heirs are obliged to pay for his foster care, in proportion to their rights to inherit from him.

Chapter

The Maintenance of Close Relatives and Slaves *[Nafaqat al-Aqārib wa 'l-Mamālīk]*

A man is obliged to provide maintenance for his parents and grandparents of any generation, and for his children and offspring of any generation. He must also provide for those entitled to inherit from him, if they are poor and he has property with which to maintain them. If a poor man has two heirs, or more, his maintenance is incumbent upon them in proportion to their rights to inherit from him, apart from the son, for his maintenance is incumbent on his father exclusively.

The owners of slaves are obliged to provide them with maintenance, and whatever they need in the way of food and clothing. If they do not provide for their slaves, they will be forced to sell them, if they insist on that.

Chapter

The Marriage Banquet
[al-Walīma]

This is the invitation to celebrate the wedding. It is a recommended practice, because Allāh's Messenger (Allāh bless him and give him peace) said to ʿAbd ar-Raḥmān ibn ʿAwf, when he informed him that he had married:

> May Allāh bless you! Provide a banquet, if only with a sheep!

Responding to the invitation is obligatory, because of the saying of Allāh's Messenger (Allāh bless him and give him peace):

> If someone does not respond, he has disobeyed Allāh and His Messenger. If someone does not wish to eat, he should invoke a blessing and depart.

As for the practice of scattering treats and picking them up from the ground, it is permissible though disapproved. If they are distributed among those present, that is more appropriate.

The Book of Foodstuffs
[Kitāb al-Aṭʿima]

The Book of Foodstuffs
[Kitāb al-Aṭ'ima]

These are of two kinds: animal and non-animal. As for non-animal foods, all of them are permissible, except those that are dirty or harmful, like poisons. All beverages are permissible, except those that are intoxicating, for they are unlawful in any quantity, small or great, and of whatever they consist, because of the saying of Allāh's Messenger (Allāh bless him and give him peace):

> Every intoxicant is unlawful, and if a large measure of something causes intoxication, a mere handful of it is unlawful. If grape juice *[khamra]* is fresh, it is pure and lawful, but if it is fermented it is not pure.

Subsection

There are two kinds of animal: aquatic and terrestrial. As for the aquatic kind, all of its species are lawful, except the snake, the frog and the crocodile. As for the terrestrial kind, the following species are unlawful:

- All predatory beasts with fangs.
- All birds with talons, like eagles, vultures and the spotted raven.
- Domestic asses and mules.
- Any beast that eats the putrid carcasses of birds.
- Creeping pests like the rat and the mouse, but not the jerboa and the lizard, because one of these was eaten at the table of Allāh's Messenger (Allāh bless him and give him peace), while he was watching. He was asked: "Is it unlawful?" and he said: "No!"

Apart from those listed above, all terrestrial animals are permissible. It is permissible to eat the flesh of horses and hyenas, because the Prophet (Allāh bless him and give him peace) allowed the consumption of horseflesh, and he called the hyena an animal to be hunted as game.

Chapter

Ritual Slaughter
[Dhakāh]

Every creature in the sea is permissible without ritual slaughter, because of the saying of Allāh's Messenger (Allāh bless him and give him peace), with reference to the sea:

> Lawful is its *maita* [meat that is not ritually slaughtered].

This does not apply to any aquatic creature that also lives on the land, for it is not permissible unless it is ritually slaughtered, apart from the scorpion and suchlike. No terrestrial creature is permissible without ritual slaughter, except the locust and suchlike.

Ritual slaughter is subdivided into three categories: *naḥr* [stabbing in the pit of the throat], *dhabḥ* [cutting the jugular vein], and *ʿaqr* [hocking, hamstringing]. Stabbing in the pit of the throat is recommended in the case of camels, and cutting the jugular vein in all other cases. It is permissible, however, if *naḥr* is used to slaughter an animal that is preferably slaughtered by *dhabḥ*, and vice versa.

For ritual slaughter in all its forms, these three preconditions are stipulated:

1. The aptitude of the butcher who performs it. In order to qualify, he must be a man of sound mind, capable of *dhabḥ*, and a Muslim or a member of a Scriptural religion. As for the child, the lunatic, the drunkard, and the unbeliever who is not a member of a Scriptural religion, the animal he slaughters is not lawful food.
2. He must mention the Name of Allāh (Exalted is He) at the time of slaughter, and when targeting hunted game, if he is endowed with the faculty of speech. If he is dumb, he must point toward heaven. If he deliberately omits the invocation of Allāh's Name

over the slaughtered animal, it is not lawful food, but if he omits it absent-mindedly, it is lawful. If he omits it over hunted game, it is not lawful, whether his omission is deliberate or absent-minded.

3. The ritual slaughter must be performed with a sharp-pointed instrument, whether it consists of iron, or stone, or cane, or anything else except the teeth and claws [of animals and birds trained for hunting], because of the saying of Allāh's Messenger (Allāh bless him and give him peace):

> If its blood has been caused to flow, and the Name of Allāh has been mentioned over it, you may eat it. But teeth and claws must not be used [as the means of slaughter].

In the case of game, the hunter is advised to shoot an arrow with a sharp point, or to dispatch a trained hunting animal or bird, and thereby wound the hunted beast. If the hunted beast is killed by a stone, or a bullet, or a snare, or if the animal or bird sent to wound the beast kills it with its impact, or by choking it, or by filling it with fear, it is not lawful food. If someone hunts with a threshing pole, he may eat what he kills with its point, but not what he kills with its blunt edge. If he plants scythes to catch game, invoking the Name of Allāh, and they wound or kill the game, it is lawful food.

Subsection

Two preconditions are stipulated for *dhabḥ* and *naḥr* in particular:

1. The incision must be made in the jugular vein and the pit of the throat, in order to sever the gullet and the esophagus, and thereby cut off all means of survival.
2. The animal to be slaughtered *[al-madhbūḥ]* must have in it a life that will be taken away by the act of slaughter *[dhabḥ]*. If it has nothing in it except the semblance of life and the signs of movement in its intestines, it is not made lawful by *dhabḥ* or by *naḥr*. If that is not the case, it is lawful, because of a traditional report from Kaʿb, who said: "We had flocks pasturing on herbage. A slave girl of ours noticed a dead sheep, so she broke a rock and used it to slaughter the animal. Allāh's Messenger (Allāh bless

him and give him peace) was asked about that, so he gave the order for it to be eaten."

As for *ʿaqr*, it is killing with a wound inflicted on a part of the body other than the jugular vein and the pit of the throat. It is prescribed for every animal that cannot be held still, including game and cattle, because of the traditional report from Abū Rāfiʿ, who said: "A camel once ran away and exhausted its pursuers, so a man shot an arrow at it and captured it. Allāh's Messenger (Allāh bless him and give him peace) then said:

> These large domestic animals have weird habits like the weird habits of wild beasts. If one of them gets the better of you, this is how you must deal with it."

If a camel falls into a well, and then, since it is impossible to slaughter it by *naḥr*, it is wounded in any part of its body and dies from the wound, it may be eaten as lawful food.

The Book of Hunted Game
[Kitāb aṣ-Ṣaid]

The Book of Hunted Game
[Kitāb aṣ-Ṣaid]

It is not permissible to eat any hunted game that can be slaughtered by *dhabḥ*, unless it has been slaughtered by that method. If it is impossible to slaughter a hunted animal by *dhabḥ*, and it dies from the wounding called *ʿaqr*, it is lawful on six preconditions, three of which we have mentioned above, in the chapter headed Ritual Slaughter *[dhakāh]*.

The fourth precondition is that the wounding must be inflicted by a trained hunting animal or bird, meaning one that chases the prey when it is dispatched, and responds to the call when it is summoned. In the case of hunting animals, especially the dog and the cheetah *[fahd]*, it is important for them not to gnaw at the prey when they seize it, but pecking is not considered important in the case of hunting birds [like the hawk and the falcon].

The fifth precondition is that the hunter must dispatch the instrument. If the dog goes chasing by itself, its prey is therefore not permissible as food.

The sixth precondition is that the hunter must deliberately target the game. If he shoots his arrow or dispatches his dog at random, without having any game in sight, and he happens to hit a game beast, it is not permissible.

Hunted game is also unlawful whenever some extraneous element participates in the hunt, and that element is not a permissible means of killing the game. For instance:

- The hunter's own dog or his own arrow is accompanied by another dog or another arrow, and he does not know who dispatched it, or does not know whether that person invoked Allāh's Name over it.
- The hunter shoots his prey with a poisoned arrow, intending to kill it, or it drowns in water, or he finds it bearing a mark, other

than the mark of the arrow or the dog, which probably indicates the cause of its death.

These rules are based on the saying of Allāh's Messenger (Allāh bless him and give him peace), reported by ʿAdī ibn Ḥātim:

> When you dispatch your trained dog, and invoke Allāh's Name over it, so it acts on your behalf and you catch the prey alive, you must slaughter the prey by *dhabḥ*. If the dog kills the prey, but does not eat any part of it, you may eat it, for its seizure by the dog is a form of ritual slaughter *[dhakāh]*. If the dog eats, you must not eat, for I am afraid that it may have been acting simply on its own behalf. If other dogs participate in the hunt, you must not eat, for you invoked Allāh's Name over your dog only, and not over any other.
>
> When you shoot your arrow, you must invoke the Name of Allāh over it. Then, if the prey is hidden from you for a day or two days, and you find nothing on it except the mark of your arrow, you may eat it if you wish. If you find it drowned in water, you must not eat it, for you do not know whether it was the water that killed it, or your arrow.

Chapter

The Case of Someone in Dire Need *[al-Muḍṭarr]*

If someone is in dire need, facing the threat of starvation, and he cannot find anything except unlawful food, he is entitled to eat enough of it to keep himself barely alive. If he finds something that is classed as unlawful by the general consensus [of the jurists], and something about which there is disagreement, he may eat some of the latter. If he finds nothing except food belonging to someone whose need for it is as urgent as his own, it is not permissible for him to take it. If its owner can manage without it, he may take it from him for its price, and if he withholds it from him, he may take it by force, then compensate him for it whenever he is able to do so. If the person in dire need is killed, he is a martyr *[shahīd]*, and his killer is liable for his indemnification, but if the withholder is killed, there is no such liability.

It is not permissible to consume forbidden food for medicinal purposes, nor for someone who is thirsty to drink alcoholic liquor. The latter is permissible, however, for the purpose of clearing a blockage from the throat, provided that no other liquid is available.

Chapter

The Solemn Vow
[an-Nadhr]

If someone vows to perform an act of worshipful obedience, its performance is incumbent upon him, because of the saying of Allāh's Messenger (Allāh bless him and give him peace):

> If someone vows that he will obey Allāh, he must obey Him!

If he is incapable of performing it, like an old man who vows a fast that he cannot keep, the expiation of an oath is incumbent upon him, because of the saying of Allāh's Messenger (Allāh bless him and give him peace):

> If someone makes a solemn vow that he cannot fulfill, its expiation is the expiation of an oath.

If someone vows that he will walk to the Sacred House of Allāh, the walk is not sufficient for him except during the Pilgrimage *[Ḥajj]* or the Visitation *[ʿUmra]*. If he is incapable of walking, he must ride.

If he vows that he will fast without interruption, but he is incapable of doing so, he must fast intermittently and make expiation. If he breaks the continuity with a valid excuse, he is free to choose between its recommencement, on the one hand, and completing the remainder and making expiation, on the other. If he breaks it without a valid excuse, its recommencement is obligatory, If he vows a specific period, but then breaks fast in the course of it, he must complete it, fulfill his vow and make expiation, in any case.

If he vows to emancipate a slave, this applies to any slave who is duly qualified, unless he intends a particular slave.

No vow may concern an act of sinful disobedience, nor something that is *mubāḥ* [indifferent; permissible but not positively recommended], nor something over which the human being has no control, nor something by which an oath *[yamīn]* is intended. This is based on the saying of Allāh's Messenger (Allāh bless him and give him peace):

> Let there be no vow about an act of sinful disobedience to Allāh, nor something over which the human being has no control.

He also said:

> Let there be no vow except about something by which one seeks the good pleasure of Allāh (Glory be to Him).

If someone makes a compound vow, in which he combines an act of worshipful obedience with something else, he is obliged to fulfill only the act of worshipful obedience, because of this report by Ibn ʿAbbās: "Allāh's Messenger (Allāh bless him and give him peace) caught sight of a man standing, so he asked about him and they said: 'Abū Isrāʾīl has vowed that he will stand in the sun, that he will not sit down, nor seek shade, nor speak, and that he will fast.' On hearing this, he said: 'Command him to speak, to seek shade, to sit down and to conclude his fast!'"

If he addresses a vow to Allāh, but does not pronounce His Name, the expiation of an oath is incumbent upon him.

The Book of Oaths
[Kitāb al-Aimān]

The Book of Oaths
[Kitāb al-Aimān]

If someone swears that he will not do something, but he does it, or that he will certainly do it at a particular time, but he does not do it at that time, the expiation of an oath is incumbent upon him, unless he says: "If Allāh wills *[in shā'a 'llāh]*" in connection with his oath, or he does it under coercion, or absent-mindedly, in which case no expiation is incumbent upon him.

No expiation is incurred by swearing about something that has passed, whether he is deliberately lying about it, or thinks that it was as he swears, but it was not so. The same applies to the oath that slips off his tongue without deliberate intent, as when he exclaims in the midst of his speech: "No, by Allāh!" and: "Yes, by Allāh!" That is because of the saying of Allāh (Exalted is He):

Allāh will not take you to task for that which is unintentional in your oaths. (2:225)	*lā yu'ākhidhu-kumu 'llāhu bi'l-laghwi fī aimāni-kum.*

Expiation is not obligatory unless the oath is sworn by invoking Allāh (Exalted is He), or one of His Names, or one of the attributes of His Essence—like His Knowledge, His Speech, His Might, His Power, His Majesty, His Promise, His Covenant and His Trustworthiness—with the exception of the vow *[nadhr]* by which an oath is intended, for its expiation is the expiation of an oath.

Even if he swears by all of this and the whole of the Qur'ān, and then breaks the oath, or repeats it with reference to one thing before the expiation, or if he swears a single oath about several things, no more than a single expiation is incumbent upon him. On the other hand, if he swears several oaths about one thing, the expiation of each oath is incumbent upon him.

If someone interprets his oath, he is entitled to its interpretation, unless the oath is sinful, in which case its interpretation is of no use to him, because of the saying of Allāh's Messenger (Allāh bless him and give him peace):

> Your oath means what your companion believes that you mean by it.

Chapter

The Construction of Oaths
[Jāmiʿ al-Aimān]

Oaths are construed by referring to the intention that is implicit in their verbal expression. For instance:

- If someone swears that he will not speak to a man, meaning one man in particular, or that he will not eat a meal, meaning a particular meal, his oath is understood in the specific sense.
- If he swears that water will not quench his thirst, meaning that he will not receive its benefit, he breaks his oath by taking anything that contains some benefit.
- If he swears that he will not wear a garment that he has woven, meaning that he will not receive its benefit, but he sells it and profits by its price, he has broken his oath.
- If he swears that he will surely fulfill someone's right tomorrow, meaning no later than tomorrow, and he fulfills it today, he has not broken his oath.
- If he swears that he will not sell his garment except for one hundred coins, but he sells it for more than that, he has not broken his oath, if he meant that he would not sell it for less than one hundred.
- If he swears that he will surely marry a second wife, with the intention of infuriating his first wife, his oath is not kept except by a marriage that infuriates her.
- If he swears that he will surely beat his wife, with the intention of causing her pain, his oath is not kept except by a beating that causes her pain. If he swears that he will surely beat her with ten lashes, but he combines them and beats her with a single blow, his oath is not kept.

If the intention is lacking, reference is made to the cause of his oath and what provoked it, for this takes the place of the intention, which it serves to indicate. If that is also lacking, his oath is construed according to the literal sense of its verbal expression.

If he uses a term defined by Islāmic law, like the ritual prayer *[ṣalāt]* and the alms-due *[zakāt]*, his oath is construed accordingly and it is taken to convey the correct meaning of the term. If he swears that he will not make a sale, and he then makes a sale that is legally invalid, his oath is not broken, unless he connects it with something that can never be sold legally, like a free man and alcoholic liquor, in which case his oath includes the form of the sale.

If he uses a term that has no legal definition, but which does have a customary meaning in ordinary usage, like *rāwiya* [a camel that carries bags of water for irrigation purposes] and *ẓaʿīna* [a camel-borne sedan chair for women], his oath is construed in that sense. If he swears that he will not mount a *dābba* [riding animal], his oath applies to horses, mules and donkeys.

If he swears that he will not savor the scent of *raiḥān*, his oath relates to the Persian meaning of the term [sweet basil]. If he uses the term *shiwāʾ*, it signifies grilled meat.

If he swears that he will not *yaṭaʾ* his wife, his oath is broken by cohabiting with her. If he swears that he will not *yaṭaʾ* a house, his oath is broken by entering it, by whatever means.

If he swears that he will not eat meat, nor a head, nor eggs, his oath applies to the meat, the head and the eggs of any animal. The term *adm* [seasoning] signifies everything with which bread is usually eaten, both liquid and solid, like meat, eggs, salt, cheese and olives.

If he swears that he will not reside in a house, his oath includes everything that is called a residence. If he has been residing in it, and he stays on after he could have departed from it, he has broken his oath. If he stays in order to move his furniture, or he swears at night and then stays until the morning, or he fears for his life so he stays until he feels safe, he has not broken his oath.

Chapter

Expiation of the Oath
[Kaffārat al-Yamīn]

[As explained in the Qur'ān] its expiation is:

The feeding of ten of the needy	*iṭ'āmu 'asharati masākīna*
with the average of that	*min awsaṭi mā tuṭ'imūna*
wherewith you feed your own folk,	*ahlī-kum*
or the clothing of them, or	*aw kiswatu-hum aw*
the liberation of a slave,	*taḥrīru raqaba:*
and if someone cannot	*fa-man lam yajid fa-ṣiyāmu*
find [the necessary means],	
let him keep a three days' fast. (5:89)	*fa-ṣiyāmu thalāthati ayyām.*

The person concerned is free to choose between making the expiation before the oath is broken, or postponing it till later, because of the saying of Allāh's Messenger (Allāh bless him and give him peace):

> If someone swears an oath, and then thinks that another is better, let him expiate his oath and let him perform the one that is better.

In another version of this report, the wording is:

> Let him perform the one that is better, and let him expiate his oath.

Where clothing is concerned, it is sufficient for him to provide the kind of attire in which performance of the ritual prayer is permissible: namely, a gown for the man, and a full dress and a veil for the woman. It is sufficient for him to feed five needy people and to clothe five. If he emancipates half of a slave, or feeds five needy people [but does not clothe them], or clothes them [but does not feed them], or emancipates half of each of two slaves, that is not sufficient for him.

The slave does not expiate except by fasting. Fasting is also the means of expiation for someone who cannot find afford any extra expense, in addition to his own sustenance, the sustenance of his family, and the payment of his debt. He is not obliged to sell anything that he needs, like a dwelling, a servant, furniture, books, utensils, and merchandise from which he must profit to meet his needs. If someone becomes wealthy after embarking on the fast, he is not obliged to change course.

If someone can find only one needy person, he must provide for him repeatedly for ten days.

The Book of Serious Crimes
[Kitāb al-Jināyāt]

The Book of Serious Crimes
[Kitāb al-Jināyāt]

Killing without legal right is subdivided into three categories:

1. Murder committed with deliberate intent *[al-ʿamd]*. This means that the killer kills his victim with a wound or any act that is likely to kill him, such as striking him once with a large marble slab, or repeatedly with a small one, or throwing him down from a towering height, or strangling him, or burning him, or drowning him, or giving him poison to drink, or giving a false testimony against him that necessitates his execution or his being sentenced to death, or something else of this kind, with deliberate intent and knowing that the victim is an inviolable human being [protected by Islāmic law]. This gives the victim's custodian the option between lethal retaliation *[qawad]* and exacting the blood money *[diya]*, because of the saying of Allāh's Messenger (Allāh bless him and give him peace):

   > If someone has custody of a murder victim, he has two options: he may either kill [the murderer], or he may accept ransom from him.

   If he spares the killer from lethal retaliation in exchange for more than a prescribed payment of blood money, that is also permissible.
2. Murder committed with quasi-deliberate intent *[shibh al-ʿamd]*. This means that the offender deliberately commits the crime against the victim, but with something that would be very unlikely to kill him. He is not subject to lethal retaliation, and the blood money must be paid by the *ʿāqila* [paternal relatives of the killer] within three years.
3. Murder committed by mistake *[al-khaṭaʾ]*. This is of two kinds:

   a) The first is committed by doing something that is not intended to kill the victim, but which results in his being killed, or which turns out to be the cause of his death, such as digging a well, for instance. As for murder committed by a sleepwalker, a minor or a lunatic, it is subject to the same ruling as murder committed with quasi-deliberate intent *[shibh al-ʿamd]*.

b) The second is committed when someone kills a Muslim in the zone of war, supposing him to be an enemy warrior, or when he aims a shot at the battle line of the unbelievers, but his arrow hits a Muslim. Expiation *[kaffāra]* without blood money is required in such cases, because of the saying of Allāh (Exalted is He):

If he be of a people hostile to you, and he is a believer, then [expiation is made by] setting free a believing slave. (4:92)	*fa-in kāna min qawmin ʿaduwwin la-kum wa huwa muʾminun fa-taḥrīru raqabatin.*

Chapter

Preconditions of the Incumbency of Retaliation *[Qiṣāṣ]* and its Execution.

The incumbency of retaliation depends on the fulfillment of four preconditions:

1. The killer must be a responsible adult. As for the minor and the lunatic, no retaliation is imposed on either of them.
2. The victim must be *maʿṣūm* [inviolable; protected by Islāmic law]. If he is an enemy warrior, or an apostate, or a killer in battle, or a married man guilty of sexual misconduct, or if the killer kills him in defense of himself, or his property, or his honor, there is no liability in such cases.
3. The victim must be of the same status [in terms of religion and liberty] as the criminal. The free Muslim is therefore killed in retaliation for the free Muslim, whether male or female, but a free man is not killed in retaliation for a slave, nor a Muslim in retaliation for an unbeliever, because of the saying of Allāh's Messenger (Allāh bless him and give him peace):

   > A believer must not be killed in retaliation for an unbeliever.

   The *dhimmī* is killed in retaliation for the *dhimmī*,[21] and the *dhimmī* is killed in retaliation for the Muslim. The slave is killed in retaliation for the slave, and the free man is killed in retaliation for the free man.

[21] A *dhimmī* is a member of the *ahl adh-dhimma*, meaning the Jewish, Christian or Sabean subjects of an Islāmic state, who, in return for the payment of a special tax, are entitled under Islāmic law to security of their persons and their property.

4. The killer must not be a father or forefather of the victim, for a progenitor is not killed in retaliation for his offspring, however many generations come between them, and both parents are alike in this respect. If the blood-custodian is an offspring, or he has any right at stake, however small, lethal retaliation is not incumbent.

Subsection

For its execution to be permissible, three preconditions are stipulated:

1. It must be assigned to a responsible person. If it is assigned to someone else, or he has any right at stake, however small, its execution is not permissible. If someone other than the responsible person fulfills his right by himself, that is satisfactory.
2. The unanimous agreement of all those entitled to its execution. If any one of them does not consent to it, or there is an absentee among their number, its execution is not permissible. If one of them does execute it [unilaterally], there is no retaliation against him, but he is liable for the outstanding blood money, and his partners are entitled to their claim on the legacy of the criminal.

   Those entitled to retaliation are all those who inherit the property [of the victim], in proportion to their inheritances.
3. Security from infringement. If the criminal is a pregnant woman, it is not permissible to execute lethal retaliation on her, nor retaliation by wounding, nor to execute a legal penalty *[ḥadd]*, until she gives birth and her child can survive without her.

Subsection

It is canceled after its incumbency by three factors:

1. The granting of exemption from it, in whole or in part. If one of the heirs waives his right, or part of it, the whole of it is canceled, and the other heirs are entitled to their rightful share of the blood money. If the exemption is granted for a financial consideration,

he is entitled to his rightful share of the blood money, but if not, he is entitled to nothing except the spiritual reward.

2. The [avenging] killer, or one of his children, would inherit something from [the shedding of] his blood.
3. The murderer dies, so lethal retaliation is canceled and the blood money is incumbent on his legacy.

If one person kills two with deliberate intent, and the custodians of the two victims agree on his being killed in retaliation for them both, he will be killed in retaliation for them both. If they disagree about the execution, he will be killed in retaliation for the first victim, and blood money will be required for the second. If the retaliation of the first is canceled, the custodians of the second are entitled to its execution.

Retaliation is normally executed by beheading with the sword, but in certain cases he may be executed in the same manner as he killed his victim.

Chapter

Collaboration in Murder
[Al-Ishtirāk fi'l-Qatl]

A group may be killed in retaliation for a single victim. If the killing of one of them is unfeasible, because of his paternal relationship, or because his status [in terms of religion and liberty] is not equal to that of the victim, or due to the granting of exemption, his partners will be killed. If one of them is not a responsible person, or he acted by mistake, lethal retaliation is not imposed on any one of them.

If a man compels a man to kill, so he kills, or one of the two inflicts a single wound and the other inflicts one hundred, or one of them cuts off [a hand] from the wrist and the other [an arm] from the elbow, they are both murderers and retaliation is incumbent on them both. If blood money is required, they are both equally liable for it. If one of them slaughters the victim [like an animal, by slicing the jugular vein], then the other cuts off his hand or slices it in half, the murderer is the first. If one of them cuts the victim, then the second slaughters him, the cutter is guilty of cutting and the slaughterer of slaughter.

If someone commands a person to kill, when that person knows that the killing is unlawful, so he kills, retaliation is incumbent on the perpetrator, and the commander is subject to chastisement. If he commands someone who does not know that it is unlawful, or who cannot tell the difference, retaliation is incumbent on the commander. If someone traps a person for the kill, so he is killed, the killer will be killed, and the trapper will be imprisoned until he dies.

Chapter

Retaliation for Wounds
[al-Qawad ʿala 'l-Jurūḥ]

For each member of the victim's body, retaliation is incumbent on the same member of the assailant's body. The eye is thus taken for the eye, the nose for the nose, and each of the following for its counterpart: the eyelid, the lip, the tongue, the tooth, the hand, the foot, the penis and the testicles, and likewise every part on which it is possible to inflict retaliation. The following preconditions must be met:

- The victim of the crime must be equal in status [in terms of religion and liberty] to the perpetrator.
- The crime must have been committed with deliberate intent.
- There must be security from the excessive mutilation caused by cutting off part of a joint, or by making the kind of incision that lays the bone bare.

As for the breaking of bones, and cuts inflicted on the forearm and the thigh, there is no retaliation in such cases, nor for a stab wound, nor for any head wound except one that simply bares the skull, unless the victim is satisfied with a superficial wound in retaliation for one that is more serious. No retaliation may be inflicted on the nose, except on the cartilagenous part, which is the soft part exclusive of the bone.

Another precondition is equivalence in the name and location [of the body part]. This means that no part may be taken from the right side or the left, or the upper region or the lower, except in retaliation for its exact equivalent. It is therefore impermissible to take fingers, or fingertips, or teeth, except in retaliation for their exact counterparts. A perfect finger may not be taken in retaliation for one that is defective, nor one that is healthy in retaliation for one that is withered. One that is defective may be taken in retaliation for one that is perfect, and one that is withered in retaliation for one that is healthy, provided there is no risk of excessive damage.

Subsection

If the wound has deprived the victim of only part of his tongue, or of the soft tip of his nose, or of his lip, or of his penal gland, or of his ear, he may take its equivalent, reckoning in fractions like half, one third and so on. If the payment of blood money is accepted [instead of physical retaliation], the victim should take a fair amount of it. If part of his tooth is broken, he may file off the same amount of the criminal's tooth, provided he is sure that it will not be unrooted. Retaliation may not be exacted for a tooth until there is no hope of its growing back, nor for a wound until it heals. Infection spreading from the retaliatiory wound does not incur compensation, but infection spreading from the criminal wound is included in the assessment of the retaliation and the blood money, unless retaliation is executed before it has healed, in which case the liability for it is canceled.

The Book of Blood Money Payments *[Kitāb ad-Diyāt]*

The Book of Blood Money Payments
[Kitāb ad-Diyāt]

The blood money *[diya]* of the free Muslim is worth one thousand measures of gold, or twelve thousand dirhams [silver coins], or one hundred camels. If the blood money is payable in compensation for a murder committed with deliberate intent *[ʿamd]*, it therefore amounts to thirty *ḥiqqa* [she-camels that are three years old], thirty *jadhaʿa* [she-camels that are four years old], and forty *khalifa*, they being pregnant she-camels. It is due immediately from the property of the murderer.

If it is payable in compensation for a murder committed with quasi-deliberate intent *[shibh al-ʿamd]*, it is the same with regard to the ages of the she-camels. It is incumbent on the *ʿāqila* [paternal relatives of the killer] within three years, one third of it at the beginning of each year.

If it is the blood money for a murder committed by mistake *[khaṭaʾ]*, it is incumbent on the *ʿāqila* on those same terms, except that it consists of twenty *bint makhāḍ* [she-camels that have been covered by a male], twenty *ibn makhāḍ* [male camels in their second year], twenty *bint labūn* [she-camels that produce milk], twenty *ḥiqqa* and twenty *jadhaʿa*.

The blood money of the free Muslim woman is half the blood money of the man. Her compensation for wounds is equal to his compensation for wounds, up to one third of the blood money, beyond which point the one-half rule applies.

The blood money of the male *Kitābī* [member of a Scriptural religion] is half the blood money of the Muslim, and their women are entitled to half that amount.

The blood money of the male *Majūsī* [Magian, Zoroastrian] is eight hundred dirhams, and their women are entitled to half that amount.

As for the blood money of the male slave and the female slave, it amounts to whatever their price may be. If part of the slave is free, it is determined by calculating the appropriate fractions of the blood money of a free man and the price of a slave.

The blood money of the child in the womb, if he is delivered dead, is the value of a precious male or female slave, whose price is five camels inherited from the stillborn child. If the pregnant woman drinks a medicine, and thereby aborts her fetus, she is liable for the value of a precious slave, and she inherits nothing. If the fetus is a *Kitābī*, the compensation is one tenth of its mother's blood money. If it is a slave, its blood money is one tenth of its mother's price. If the fetus is delivered alive, but then dies from being slapped, its blood money is the full amount, provided that its delivery occurred at a time when a similar infant would normally survive.

Chapter

The ʿĀqila and their Liabilities

The ʿāqila are the paternal relatives of the killer, all of them, whether they are closely or distantly related, as well as their patrons, except the minor, the lunatic, the pauper, and anyone whose religion is different from the killer's religion. In assessing the liability of each one of them, reference must be made to the independent judgment of the Imām, who will prescribe for him an amount that is convenient and not troublesome. Whatever is left over is incumbent on the killer, as in the case of one who has no ʿāqila to contribute blood money.

The ʿāqila are not liable for blood money if the murder was committed with deliberate intent, nor if the victim was a slave, nor in cases involving agreed settlement or acknowledgment, nor for anything less than one third of the total amount.

Protected non-Muslims *[ahl-dhimma]*[22] share with one another in the payment of blood money, but there is no support from the ʿāqila for an apostate, nor for someone who embraced Islām after committing his crime, or whose relationship was brought to light only after its commission.

Subsection

The crime committed by the slave is upon his own shoulders, unless the master ransoms him with the lesser of two amounts: the blood money due, or his price. For the crime committed against him, the blood money is the amount by which, in relation to the wealth of the criminal, his value is diminished.

[22] See note 21 on p. 279 above.

The criminal conduct of domestic animals is committed with impunity, unless they are under the control of a human being, like the rider, the guide and the driver, for he is held responsible for any damage they cause with their forelegs or their mouths, but not for what they cause with their hind legs or their tails. If he trespasses with them under his control into someone else's property, or a road, he is liable for all their criminal conduct. As for any crops they destroy by day, he is not held liable for compensation, unless they are under his control, but he is held liable for what they destroy by night.

Chapter

Blood Money Payments for Wounds
[Diyāt al-Jurūḥ]

[In compensation for wounding,] there is a prescribed payment of blood money for every part of the human being that constitutes a single organ or faculty, such as his tongue, his nose, his penis, his hearing, his sight, his sense of smell, his mind, his speech, his strength and his ability to walk. The same applies to every wound that distorts his face, that disfigures his face and his cheeks, that loosens his bladder or his bowels, and that damages his head and his beard.

As for those parts of his body that exist in pairs, there is a payment of blood money prescribed for the pair, and half of it for one of the two, such as the eyes, the eyebrows, the lips, the ears, the jawbones, the hands, the breasts, the buttocks, the testicles, the labia majora of the vulva, and the legs and feet.

There is also blood money for the four eyelids, as well as for their lashes. One quarter of it is due for each eyelid, so, if the criminal tears them out with their lashes, one full payment of blood money is incumbent.

There is blood money for the fingers of the hand, and blood money for the toes of the feet, one tenth of the total for each finger or toe. For each tip of a finger or toe, there is one third of the blood money prescribed for the whole finger or toe, except the tips of the thumbs and big toes, for which the amount is one half of the total prescribed for the whole thumb or big toe.

For each tooth the blood money is five camels.

For the soft tip of the nose, the nipple of a woman's breast, the palm of the hand, the sole of the foot, the head of the penis, and the visible part of the tooth, the blood money is that of the whole organ. In each of these cases, the blood money for partial damage is determined by fractional calculation.

For the withered hand, foot, or penis, the penis of the castrate and the impotent, the tongue of the dumb mute, the cloudy eye, the black tooth, the penis without its head, the woman's breast without its nipple, the nose without its tip, extra fingers or toes, and suchlike, the blood money is decided by the ruling of a judge.

As for the withered nose and ear, the nose of someone suffering nasal congestion and unable to smell, and the ear of the deaf, their blood money is complete.

Chapter

Head and Face Wounds *[Shijāj]* etc.

The term *shijāj* signifies wounds inflicted on the head and the face. There are nine of them:

1. The *ḥāriṣa* is one that merely scratches the skin, without drawing any blood.
2. The *bāẓila* is one that causes a split from which a slight trace of blood flows.
3. The *bāḍiʿa* is one that cuts into the flesh beneath the skin.
4. The *mutalāḥima* is one that slices the flesh.
5. The *simḥāq* is one that cuts very close to the bone.
6. The *mūḍiḥa* is one that reaches the bone. The blood money for it is five camels and it is subject to retaliation, if it is inflicted with deliberate intent.
7. The *hāshima* is one that reaches the bone and fractures it. The blood money for it is ten camels.
8. The *munaqqila* is one that reaches the bones, fractures them and dislocates them. The blood money for it is fifteen camels.
9. The *maʾmūma* is one that reaches the skin of the brain. The blood money for it is one third of the fullest amount.

For the *jāʾifa*, which is a wound that reaches the abdomen *[jawf]*, the blood money is one third of the fullest amount. If it comes out from another side of the body, it counts as two *jāʾifa*'s.

For a wound to the rib, the blood money is one camel; to the collar-bones, two camels; to the bones of the forearms, four camels.

As for other types of wounds, for which no specific payment of blood money is prescribed, explicitly or implicitly, the amount is determined by the ruling of a judge.

Chapter

The Expiation of Killing
[Kaffārat al-Qatl]

If someone kills a believer, or a *dhimmī* [non-Muslim protected by Islāmic law], without right, or he participates in the killing or in the abortion of a fetus, an expiation is incumbent upon him: namely, the emancipation of a believing slave. If that is unfeasible, he must fast for two consecutive months, as an act of repentance to Allāh, whether he is or is not a responsible adult, and whether he is a free man or a slave.

If two persons clash in combat, and they both die, an expiation is incumbent on each one of them, and his companion's blood money is incumbent on his *ʿāqila* [paternal relatives]. If they are both cavaliers, and both their horses die, each of them is obliged to make compensation for the other's horse. If one of them is standing still and the other is mobile, the one who is mobile is obliged to make compensation for the riding beast of the one who is standing still, and his blood money is incumbent on his *ʿāqila*, unless the one who is standing still is a trespasser, like someone sitting on a narrow road, or on another person's property, in which case he is liable for an expiation and compensation for the riding animal of the one who is mobile, and nothing is incumbent on the one who is mobile, nor on his *ʿāqila*. If three men shoot with a catapult, and the stone kills a person who is *maʿṣūm* [inviolable; protected by Islāmic law], each one of them is liable for an expiation, and one third of the blood money is incumbent on the *ʿāqila* of each one of them. If one of the three is killed, the same rule applies, except that one third of the blood money is canceled. If they are more than three, the share of the one killed is canceled, and the remainder of the blood money is incumbent on the properties of the survivors.

Chapter

The Oath taken by Fifty Persons *[Qasāma]*

As related by Sahl ibn Abī Ḥathma and Rāfi' ibn Khadīj, Muḥayyiṣa and 'Abdu'llāh ibn Sahl set out before [the battle of] Khaibar, and they became separated among the date palms. 'Abdu'llāh ibn Sahl was then killed, so they suspected the Jews. Allāh's Messenger (Allāh bless him and give him peace) said:

> Let fifty of you take an oath against a man among them.

They said: "It is a matter we did not witness, so how can we swear?" He said:

> Then let the Jews exculpate you with the oaths of fifty of them.

They said: "[They are] an unbelieving people," so the Prophet (Allāh bless him and give him peace) paid his blood money.

When a man is found killed, so his custodians accuse the local inhabitants of his murder, and there is enmity and malevolence between them—as there was between the Helpers *[Anṣār]* and the people of Khaibar—the custodians may swear fifty oaths against one of them and become entitled to his blood. If they do not swear, the accused may swear fifty oaths and be acquitted. If they refrain, they are obliged to pay the blood money. If the claimants do not swear, and they are not satisfied with the oath of the accused, the Imām will pay his ransom from the public treasury. They may not swear against more than one person. If there is no enmity between them and no malevolence, the accused may swear a single oath and be acquitted.

The Book of Legal Penalties *[Kitāb al-Ḥudūd]*

The Book of Legal Penalties
[Kitāb al-Ḥudūd]

The legal penalty *[ḥadd]* is not imposed unless the offender is a sane and responsible person *[mukallaf]*, aware of the prohibition he has violated. It is not inflicted by anyone other than the ruling authority *[imām]* or his deputy, except in the case of the slave master, for he is entitled to inflict on his slave the penalty of flogging, exclusively, because of the saying of Allāh's Messenger (Allāh bless him and give him peace):

> If the female slave of one of you is guilty of sexual misconduct, let him flog her.

The master is not entitled to subject his slave to amputation for theft, nor to kill him for apostasy [from Islām], nor to flog his *mukātab* [slave he has promised to emancipate for an agreed price], nor to flog his female slave who is married. Where flogging is concerned, the penalty imposed on the slave is half the penalty imposed on the free man. If someone confesses a punishable offense, but then withdraws his confession, the penalty lapses.

Subsection

Flogging must be administered with a whip that is neither brand-new nor worn and frayed. The person flogged must not be stretched out, nor tied up, nor stripped naked. His face, his head and his private parts must be protected. A man must be beaten while standing upright, and a woman while sitting down. A woman's clothes must fit her tightly, and her hands must be held. In the case of a person who is sick, and whose recovery can be expected, the flogging should be postponed until he recovers, because of the following report from ʿAlī (may Allāh be well pleased with him), who said: "A female slave of Allāh's Messenger (Allāh bless him and give him peace) was guilty of sexual misconduct, so he commanded me to flog her. As it turned out, she was in the early stage of pregnancy, so I was afraid that I might kill her if I flogged her. I mentioned that to the Prophet (Allāh bless him and give him peace), and he said: "You have done well!" If the invalid is not expected to recover, and the whip is considered too dangerous for him, he should be flogged one time only, with a bundle containing as many sticks as the number of floggings prescribed for his offense.

Subsection

If several penalties are owed to Allāh (Exalted is He), including a lethal execution, the offender is put to death and the other penalties are dropped. If he has committed sexual misconduct or theft on several occasions, but has not been punished, a single penalty should be enforced. If several different penalties are incurred, of kinds in which lethal execution is not included, all of them should be enforced in order of severity, beginning with the lightest. Legal penalties are averted by uncertainties, so they would not be enforced in cases like the following:

- If a man committed fornication with a slave girl in whom he owned a share, however small, or in whom his son owned a share.
- If he consummated a marriage that was subject to dispute, or did so by coercion.
- If he stole from property in which he or his son had a rightful claim, provided the amount taken was less than the total wealth of his debtor who was unable to repay him his due.

Subsection

If someone incurs a legal penalty outside the Sacred Precinct, then takes refuge inside the Sacred Precinct, or if refuge is taken therein by someone who is subject to retaliation *[qiṣāṣ]*,[23] he enjoys immunity until he comes out. He must not engage in buying or selling, however. If he does that inside the Sacred Precinct, the penalty will be exacted from him therein. If someone incurs a legal penalty in the course of a military campaign, it will not be exacted until he emerges from the sphere of combat.

[23] The Islāmic law of retaliation *[qiṣāṣ]* is based on the verse *[āya]* of the Qur'ān in which Allāh (Almighty and Glorious is He) has told us:

And We prescribed for them therein	*wa katabnā ʿalai-him fī-hā*
[in the Torah]: "A life for a life,	*anna 'n-nafsa bi 'n-nafsi, wa*
an eye for an eye, a nose for a nose,	*wa 'l-ʿaina bi 'l-ʿaini wa 'l-anfa bi' l-anfi*
an ear for an ear,	*wa 'l-udhuna bi'l-udhuni*
a tooth for a tooth and for wounds retaliation."	*wa's-sinna bi 's-sinni wa 'l-jurūḥa qiṣāṣ :*
But if anyone forgoes it as a freewill offering,	*fa-man taṣaddaqa bi-hi fa-huwa*
that shall be an expiation for him.	*kaffāratun la-h. wa man lam yaḥkum*
Whoever judges not by that which Allāh	*bi-mā anzala 'llāhu*
has revealed: such are wrong-doers. (5:45)	*fa-ulā'ika humu 'ẓ-ẓālimūn.*

Chapter

The Legal Penalty for Sexual Misconduct *[Ḥadd az-Zinā]*

If someone commits sexual obscenity in the front part or the backside of a woman he does not possess, or of a young man, or of anyone with whom he does that, his penalty is stoning, if he is a *muḥṣan* [see * below], or one hundred strokes of flogging and exile for a year, if he is not a *muḥṣan*. That is because of the saying of Allāh's Messenger (Allāh bless him and give him peace):

> Take it from me that Allāh has prescribed a way of dealing with them: For the virgin [who fornicates] with the virgin, [the penalty is] one hundred strokes of flogging and exile for a year, and for the non-virgin [who fornicates] with the non-virgin, [the penalty is] stoning.

*The muḥṣan is a free adult who has had sexual intercourse with a wife like himself in these attributes [of freedom and adulthood], in her vulva or vagina, during a valid marriage. Sexual misconduct *[zinā]* is not established except by one of two things: (1) Its being confessed four times, with explicit mention of its actual nature. (2) The testimony of four men, free and of good reputation, who describe the sexual misconduct, give evidence at a single session, and concur in testifying to a single act of sexual misconduct.

Chapter

The Legal Penalty for Slander *[Ḥadd al-Qadhf]*

If someone accuses a *muḥṣan* of sexual misconduct, or bears witness to it against him, and the evidence is imperfect, he is subject to eighty strokes of flogging, if the slandered person demands it. The *muḥṣan* is a free man, an adult, a Muslim, intelligent and chaste. The legal penalty is inflicted on someone who slanders the *mulāʿana* [woman accused of adultery by her husband] or her son. If someone slanders a group with a single statement, he is subject to a single penalty, if it is demanded by all of them or any one of them. If one of them pardons him, the right of the others is not canceled.

Chapter

The Legal Penalty for Drinking Alcoholic Liquor *[Ḥadd al-Muskir]*

If someone drinks alcoholic liquor, whether little or much, of his own volition and knowing that much of it is intoxicating, his legal penalty is forty strokes of flogging. That is because ʿAlī (may Allāh be well pleased with him) flogged al-Walīd ibn ʿUqba with forty strokes for drinking wine, and he said: "The Prophet inflicted forty strokes [in such cases], Abū Bakr inflicted forty, and ʿUmar inflicted eighty. Each is an acceptable practice, and this is preferable to me." It is makes no difference whether the alcoholic liquor is the juice of grapes or something else. If someone commits unlawful acts for which there are no specific legal penalties, he may not be flogged with more than ten strokes. That is because, as reported by Abū Burda, Allāh's Messenger (Allāh bless him and give him peace) once said:

> No one should be flogged with more than ten strokes, except for incurring one of Allāh's legal penalties, unless he has sexual intercourse with his wife's slave girl, without her permission, in which case he should be flogged with one hundred strokes.

Chapter

The Legal Penalty for Theft
[Ḥadd as-Sariqa]

If someone steals one quarter of a dīnār [gold coin] in cash, or three dirhams [silver coins] in paper money, or the equivalent of either in whatever form of property, and removes it from its place of safekeeping, his right hand should be amputated from the joint of the wrist, and then cauterized. If he relapses into theft, his left foot should be amputated from the joint of the ankle, and then cauterized. If he relapses yet again, he should be imprisoned, for no more than one hand and one foot may be amputated.

Theft is not established except by the testimony of two reputable witnesses, or a confession made twice. Amputation must not be performed until the victim demands his property. If he gives it to the thief or sells it to him before that, the amputation is canceled, but it is not canceled thereafter. If the value of the stolen property falls short of the *niṣāb* [amount subject to the alms-due] after the theft, the amputation is not canceled. If its value was less than that beforehand, however, amputation is not required. When he has suffered amputation, the thief is obliged to return the stolen property, if it is still in good condition, or its value if it is damaged.

Chapter

The Legal Penalty imposed on Brigands
[Ḥadd al-Muḥāribīn]

They are the villains who hold people up in the desert, with the deliberate intention of seizing their possessions. If one of them commits murder and also seizes property, he should be killed and crucified, so that he becomes notorious, then turned over to his family. If one of them commits murder but does not seize property, he should be killed but not crucified. If one of them seizes property but does not commit murder, his right hand and his left foot should be amputated on the same occasion, and both should be cauterized. Amputation should not be inflicted except on one who seizes the equivalent of that for which the thief suffers amputation. If someone makes people afraid of traveling, but does not commit murder and does not seize property, he should be banished from the land. If someone repents before he is captured by force, the penalties of Allāh (Exalted is He) cease to apply to him, and he must fulfill the rightful claims of human beings, unless he is granted exemption from them.

Subsection

If someone is confronted by a villain who intends to take his life, or his property, or his wife, or by one who holds a weapon against him, or by one who enters his house without his permission, he is entitled to repel him by the easiest possible means of self-defense. If he can only defend himself by killing him, he is entitled to kill him, without incurring any liability. If the defender is killed, he is a martyr *[shahīd]*, and his killer is held responsible for him. If someone is attacked by a domestic animal, he is entitled to repel it in similar fashion, and no liability is incurred by so doing. If someone peers into a person's house or apartment, through a crack in the door or something of the sort, the owner incurs no liability if he throws a pebble at him and knocks out his eye. If someone bites a person's hand, so he snatches it away from him, and the biter's front teeth fall out, no liability is incurred.

Chapter

Fighting against Rebel Insurgents *[Qitāl Ahl al-Baghy]*

They are those who engage in rebellion against the Imām [Head of the Community], seeking to remove him from his office. It is incumbent on the Muslims to assist their Imām in warding them off, by the easiest possible means of defense. If he resorts to fighting them, or destroying their property, nothing is held against the defender. If the defender is killed, he is a martyr *[shahīd]*. If one of the rebels retreats, he should not be pursued. If one of them is wounded, he should not be finished off with the coup de grâce. No property of theirs should be taken as booty. No children of theirs should be held in captivity. If one of the rebels is killed, he should be properly washed and shrouded for burial, and the funeral prayer should be performed over him. No liability is incurred, by either of the two parties, for any damage they cause in the state of war, whether it be to person or property. Whatever is collected by the rebels in their state of insurrection, in the form of alms-due *[zakāt]*, or land-tax *[jizya]*, or poll-tax *[kharāj]*,[24] it does not accrue to them, nor to those who make such payments to them. As for the judgment of their judge, nothing is abrogated unless it would also be abrogated in the case of any other judge.

[24] In the technical vocabulary of Islāmic jurisprudence, the term *kharāj* means "the poll-tax paid by the *ahl adh-dhimma*, i.e., the Jewish, Christian or Sabean subjects of an Islamic state, who, in return for the payment of this special tax, are entitled under Islāmic law to security of their persons and their property."

Chapter

The Legal Ruling on the Apostate *[Ḥukm al-Murtadd]*

If someone apostatizes from Islām, whether it be a man or a woman, the penalty of death must be enforced, because of the saying of Allāh's Messenger (Allāh bless him and give him peace):

> If someone changes his religion, you must kill him.

The apostate should not be killed until he has been invited three times to repent. If he repents [he is spared], but if not, he is killed by the sword. If someone denies Allāh's existence, or attributes to Him a partner, or a consort, or a son, or if he accuses Allāh (Exalted is He) of telling lies, or blasphemes Him, or if he calls His Messenger a liar, or insults him, or if he denies a Prophet, or denies the Book of Allāh or anything from it, or denies one of the basic pillars of Islām, or if he attributes lawfulness to something declared unlawful by the consensus of legal opinion, he is guilty of apostasy—unless he is one of those who are unaware of the religious duties and prohibitions, in which case he must be informed thereof, and if he does not accept, he is guilty of unbelief.

The Islām of the intelligent minor is considered authentic. If he apostatizes, he must not be killed until he has been invited to repent, three times after his adolescence. If someone's apostasy is established, but he professes Islām, it is accepted of him. In his profession of Islām, it is sufficient for him to bear witness that there is no god but Allāh, and that Muḥammad is Allāh's Messenger, unless his unbelief takes the form of denying a Prophet, or a Book, or an obligatory religious duty, or something of the kind, or he is convinced that Muḥammad (Allāh bless him and give him peace) was sent to the Arabs exclusively, in which case it is not accepted of him until he affirms wha the has denied.

If two spouses both apostatize, and they settle in the region of war and are taken captive, their enslavement is not permissible, nor is the enslavement of a child born to them before their apostasy, but the enslavement of the rest of their children is permissible.

The Book of the Holy War
[Kitāb al-Jihād]

The Book of the Holy War
[Kitāb al-Jihād]

The holy war *[jihād]* is a collective duty *[farḍ kifāya]*.[25] If it is undertaken by those who are sufficiently qualified, it is not incumbent on the rest. It is specifically incumbent on someone who is present in the line of battle, or whose town is besieged by the enemy, but only if he is a free, adult, intelligent and capable male. The holy war is the most meritorious form of voluntary service, because, according to Abū Huraira (may Allāh be well pleased with him), Allāh's Messenger (Allāh bless him and give him peace) was asked: "Which of all deeds is the most meritorious?" and he replied:

> Belief in Allāh.

When the questioner asked: "Then which?" he said:

> The holy war in the cause of Allāh, then a pilgrimage that is blessed with acceptance *[ḥajj mabrūr]*.

According to Abū Sa'īd, Allāh's Messenger (Allāh bless him and give him peace) was asked: "Which of all people is the most meritorious?" and he replied:

> A man who wages the holy war in the cause of Allāh, with his property and in person.

The military campaign at sea is more meritorious than the military campaign on land. The holy warrior must fight together with every fellow combatant, whether he be righteous or licentious, and every group must do battle with those enemies who come close to them.

[25] In Islāmic jurisprudence, a distinction is drawn between *farḍ 'ain*, i.e., a religious duty that is incumbent on every individual Muslim, and *farḍ kifāya*, meaning a collective duty, incumbent on the Islāmic community as a whole, though not on every individual Muslim.

The full period of active duty *[ribāṭ]* is forty days, and the Prophet (Allāh bless him and give him peace) is reported as having said:

> One day of active duty in Allāh's cause is better than a thousand days in any other cause.
>
> One day of active duty in Allāh's cause is better than fasting and keeping night vigil for a month. If someone dies while on active duty, He will reward him until the Day of Resurrection, and he will be kept safe from the Tempter.

If one of his parents is alive, and a Muslim, a person must not wage the holy war without that parent's permission, unless it is specifically incumbent upon him. None of the women may enter the region of war, except a woman who is advanced in age, for the purpose of providing water and treating the wounded. The help of a polytheist *[mushrik]* may not be enlisted, except in a case of urgent need. Waging the holy war is not permissible without the consent of the commander *[amīr]*, except by those who are threatened by an enemy whose ferocity is terrifying, or who are presented with an opportunity they are afraid of missing. When they enter the region of war, it is not permissible for anyone to leave the army for the purpose of obtaining fodder, or gathering firewood, or anything of the kind, except with the commander's permission.

If someone acquires something from the region of war, and its value is such that its appropriation is not permissible for him, apart from food and fodder, he is entitled to take from it as much as he needs. If he sells it, he must return its price to the person from whom it was plundered. If part of it is still with him after his return to his home town, he is obliged to return it, unless it is a trivial amount, in which case he is entitled to consume it or give it away.

It is permissible to launch a surprise attack on the unbelievers, to shoot missiles at them with the catapult, and to fight them before declaring war on them. That is because the Prophet (Allāh bless him and give him peace) attacked the tribe of the Bani'l-Muṣṭaliq while they were unprepared, and their cattle were taking water, so he killed their warriors and took their children into captivity. It is not permissible to kill a minor among the unbelievers, nor a lunatic, nor a woman, nor a monk, nor a senile old man, nor a chronic invalid, nor a blind man, nor those who have no common sense, unless they fight.

As for the treatment of men who are taken prisoner, the Imām is free to choose between killing, enslavement, ransom and benevolence. Whatever choice he makes, however, it must be in the best interest of the Muslims. If he enslaves them, or ransoms them for property, it is a form of booty. No separation may be made between prisoners of war who are closely related, unless they are adults. If someone purchases one of them on the understanding that he is closely related to another, and the opposite comes to light, the buyer must return the extra payment made on account of the separation.

If someone is given something to help him in his military campaigning, he is entitled to keep whatever is left when he returns, unless it was not given for a particular expedition, in which case he must apply the surplus to future campaigning. If he is carried on a horse in the cause of Allāh, it belongs to him when he returns, unless it is dedicated to service in combat. Whatever he takes from the properties of the Muslims, he must return it to them, if its owner is known to him before the distribution [of booty]. If he distributes before knowing the owner, the latter is entitled to receive it for the price he charges to its taker. If one of the citizens receives it for a price, its owner is entitled to take it for its price, but if he receives it for nothing, he must simply return it to its owner. If someone purchases a captive from the enemy, the captive is obliged to repay the price for which he purchased him.

Chapter

The Spoils of War
[al-Anfāl]

These are the surplus over and above the duly allotted portion of booty, and they are of three types:

1. The plunder of the slain is not restricted to one fifth for the slayer, because of the saying of Allāh's Messenger (Allāh bless him and give him peace):

   If someone slays a man in battle, he is entitled to his plunder, that being whatever he has on him in the way of clothing, jewelry and weapons, as well as his horse with its equipment. He is only entitled to this if he kills him in the state of active warfare, not as a wounded man and not as one who is prevented from fighting.

2. The commander may grant spoils to those who benefit the Muslims, without any precondition, just as the Prophet (Allāh bless him and give him peace) gave Salama ibn Akwaʿ the portion of a cavalryman and a foot soldier, on the day of Dhū Qarad. Abū Bakr (may Allāh be well pleased with him) also granted him as spoils a woman from among the occupants of nine houses, whom he [Salama ibn Akwaʿ] brought to him one night.
3. As for what is awarded on the fulfillment of a precondition, it is of two kinds: (1) The commander says: "If someone enters the tunnel, or climbs the wall, he is entitled to such-and-such, and if someone brings ten cows or other such beasts, he is entitled to one of them." (2) The commander dispatches one raiding party in the initial advance, and assigns to it one quarter of the spoils, then dispatches another during the withdrawal, and assigns to it one third. He extracts one fifth of whatever is brought back, then gives the squadron what he assigned to it, and distributes the remainder to the army and the raiding party together.

Subsection

The commander gives small presents to those who have no allotted share of the spoils, such as women, minors, slaves and unbelievers. He grants them these gifts in proportion to their usefulness [in combat]. The pedestrian among them does not receive as much as the share of the infantryman, nor does the rider receive as much as the share of the cavalryman. If the servant goes into battle on a horse belonging to his master, the horse's share is allotted to his master, while the servant receives a small present.

Chapter

The Booties of War *[al-Ghanā'im]* and their Distribution

These are of two kinds:

1. The land. The Imām is free to choose between distributing it and establishing it as a religious endowment *[waqf]* for the Muslims. He may make it subject to a permanent land tax, payable as an annual fee by the person who has the use of it. It is not permissible to alter or sell what the Imāms establish as endowments of this type.
2. Other properties. These are allotted to anyone who engages in military action, among those who are capable of fighting and prepare for it, including merchants and others, whether he actually fights or not. The allotment depends on the condition in which he engages in military action, according to whether he is a cavalryman or a foot soldier, a slave, a Muslim or an unbeliever. No consideration is given to any previous or subsequent factors.

No allotment is due to someone who is incapable of fighting because of sickness or for some other reason, nor to someone who arrives after the war is finished, as a reinforcement or in some other capacity. If the Imām sends someone away from the action, on a mission for the welfare of the army, he must allot him a share of the booty. The army must share with its raiding parties in the booty they acquire, and they must share with the army in the booty it acquires.

The Imām must begin by extracting enough of the booty to provide for its safekeeping, its transport and other necessities. Then he must deliver the plundered goods to their owners and the prizes to those entitled to them. He must then divide the remainder into five parts, and distribute it in five shares: (1) a share for Allāh (Exalted is He) and His Messenger (Allāh bless him and give him peace, to be spent on weapons, horses and mules, and useful purposes; (2) a share for the relatives [of the Prophet (Allāh bless him and give him peace)], they being the members of [the tribes of] the Banū Hāshim and Banu'l-Muṭṭalib, whether they be rich or poor, with the male receiving the portion of two females; (3) a share for the orphans and the paupers; (4) a share for the wretched; (5) a share for the wayfarers. Then he must extract the rest of the spoils *[anfāl]* and the small gifts. He must then distribute what is left, one share to the foot soldier and three shares to the cavalryman—one share to the latter and two shares to his horse, because Ibn ʿUmar reported that Allāh's Messenger (Allāh bless him and give him peace) assigned two shares to the horse and one share to his owner. If the horse is not Arabian, it is entitled to one share and its owner to one share. If a man has two horses with him, shares are allotted to them both, but no shares are allotted to more than two horses. No shares are allotted to any riding beasts other than horses.

Subsection

As for what is abandoned by the unbelievers when they flee in panic, without needing to be pursued with horses or other riding beasts, or what is taken from them without fighting, it is a *faiʾ* [booty obtained without effort] to be spent on the welfare of the Muslims. If someone finds an unbeliever straying from the road, or wandering anywhere in the domain of Islām, so he captures him, the prisoner belongs to him. If a group of people enter without resistance into the land of war, acting stealthily without the Imām's permission, whatever they seize belongs to them, after the fifth part has been deducted.

Chapter

The Assurance of Safety *[al-Amān]*

If someone says to a warrior: "I have granted you asylum," or, "I have assured your safety," or, "No harm will come to you," or something to this effect, he has assured his safety. The assurance of safety is valid from every Muslim possessing a sound mind and the freedom of choice, whether he be free or a slave, and whether he be a man or a woman, because of the saying of Allāh's Messenger (Allāh bless him and give him peace):

> The believers are equal with regard to [retaliation for the shedding of] their blood, and the lowliest of them must strive for their protection.

The assurance of safety is valid when granted by ordinary individuals to a small community, when granted by the commander to the district of which he is in charge, and when granted by the Imām to all the unbelievers. If someone enters their home while assuring them of safety, he has assured them of safety from himself. If they release a prisoner from us, on condition that he sends them a specific sum of money, he is obliged to fulfill his promise to them. If they also stipulate that he must come back to them if he cannot pay, he is likewise obliged to fulfill his promise to them. This does not apply to a woman, however, so she is not obliged to return to them.

Subsection

It is permissible to conclude a truce with the unbelievers, provided the Imām considers it advantageous. Contracting with them is not permissible except on the part of the Imām or his deputy. He is obliged to ensure their protection from the Muslims, with the exception those at war. If he fears violation of the contract on their part, he should renounce their contract. If other unbelievers take them into captivity, it is not permissible for us to purchase their release. Exile is strictly necessary in the case of someone who is incapable of displaying his religion in the region of war, and it is recommended even for someone who is capable thereof. Exile should not be concluded so long as the unbelievers are being fought, except from a district after its conquest.

Chapter

The Tax called the *Jizya*

The tax called the *jizya* is not exacted from anyone except the People of the Scripture, they being the Jews and all who profess belief in the Torah, the Christians and all who profess belief in the Gospel, and the Magians or Zoroastrians, provided they assume the responsibility for paying the *jizya* and observing the rules of religious community. If they request that responsibility, their request must be granted, and it is unlawful to fight them. The *jizya* is collected at the start of each year, in the amount of forty-eight dirhams [silver coins] from the affluent, twenty-four dirhams from the person of moderate means, and twelve dirhams from someone of less wealth. No *jizya* is imposed on a minor, nor a woman, nor a senile old man, nor a chronic invalid, nor a blind man, nor a slave, nor a pauper who is incapable of paying it. If someone accepts Islām after the *jizya* has become due, it ceases to be required of him. If he dies, it is taken from his heritage. If one of them travels on business to another country, then returns, half of the tithe is exacted from him. If a warrior merchant enters our region, the tithe is exacted from him. If someone violates the contract, by rejecting the obligation to pay the *jizya* and observe the rules of the religious community, or by fighting the Muslims, or by fleeing to the region of war, his blood and his property become lawful. The contract of his wives and his children is not violated by his violation, unless he takes them with him to the region of war.

The Book of Judgeship
[Kitāb al-Qaḍāʾ]

The Book of Judgeship
[Kitāb al-Qaḍā']

Judgeship is a collective duty *[farḍ kifāya]*.[26] The Imām is obliged to appoint someone in whom he has confidence to perform the office of judgeship, and it is incumbent on anyone who is qualified for it, if it is requested of him and no one else is available. If someone else is available, his best course is to abstain from it. To qualify as a judge, a person must be a free man, a Muslim, attentive and discerning, well-spoken, equitable and learned. It is not permissible for him to accept a bribe, or a gift from someone who has not been in the habit of giving him presents, nor to pass judgment before knowing the truth. If he has difficulty in reaching a verdict, he should take counsel on the problem with knowledgeable and trustworthy people. He must not pass judgment while he is angry, nor in a state that prevents complete consideration. He must not admit a doorman into the court proceedings, and he must treat the two litigants with equal fairness in access to his presence, attending the session and stating their case.

[26] See note 25 on p. 313 above.

Chapter

The Nature of the Court Proceedings *[Ṣifat al-Ḥukm]*

When the two litigants are seated in the judge's presence, and one of them makes his claim against the other, the claim will not be heard unless it is presented in a document known to the accused. If it is a debt, the claimant must state its amount and its category. If it is piece of property, he must state its location and its extent. If it is an item that is present, he must point to it. If it is absent, he must state its category and its value. Then he must say to his adversary: "What do you say?" If he admits the charge, the verdict will be in favor of the claimant. If he denies it, only three situations are possible:

1. The disputed propety is in the possession of one of them, so the judge will say to the claimant: Have you any proof?" If he says yes, and establishes his proof, the verdict will be in his favor on the strength thereof. If he has no proof, the judge will say [to the other party]: "You are entitled to demand his oath." If he demands it, the judge will make him swear, and he will then acquitted, because of the saying of Allāh's Messenger (Allāh bless him and give him peace):

   > If people were [automatically] granted their claim, some folk would claim the blood of men and their properties, but the oath is incumbent on the accused.

   If he refrains from taking the oath and passes it to the claimant, the latter is required to swear and the verdict will be in his favor [if he does so]. If he also refrains, the judge will dismiss them both. If each of them has a convincing proof, the verdict will be in favor of the claimant on the strength thereof. If the holder affirms that ownership belongs to a third party, the latter becomes the litigant in the case, taking the place of the holder in the process we have described.

2. The disputed property is in the possession of both parties, so if one of them has proof the verdict will be in his favor on the strength thereof. If neither of them has any proof, or they have two proofs, the disputed object will be divided between them, and each of them must swear that he is entitled to the half assigned to him by the verdict. If one of them claims it all, and the other claims half of it, but there is no proof, it will be divided between them, and the oath is incumbent on the one who claims the half. If they have two proofs, the verdict will be in favor of the one who claims the whole.
3. The disputed property is in the possession of a third party. If he affirms that it belongs to one of the two, or to yet another owner, the person acknowledged becomes like the holder. If he affirms that it belongs to them both, it becomes like that which is in the possession of both. If he says: "I do not recognize either of them as its owner," and one of them has proof, it belongs to him. If neither of them has any proof, or each of them has proof, them must draw lots on oath. The one whose lots comes out will then swear [that he is the rightful owner], and he will take the disputed property.

Chapter

Concerning the Conflict of Claims
[Taʿāruḍ ad-Daʿāwī]

If two parties contest each other's right to a shirt that is worn by one of them, while the other is holding its sleeve, it belongs to its wearer. If they contest each other's right to a beast that one of them is riding, or on which he is carrying a load, it belongs to him. If they contest each other's right to a plot of land on which there are trees or a building, or to a farm that is cultivated by one of them, it belongs to him.

If two craftsmen contest each other's right to the equipment in a workshop, the tool of each craft belongs to its practitioner. If two spouses contest each other's right to the furniture of the house, the husband is entitled to that which is useful to men, while the wife is entitled to that which is useful to women, as well as to that which is useful to them both. If two parties contest each other's right to a wall that is attached to both of their buildings, or detached from them both, it is their common property. If it is attached to the building of one of them only, it belongs to him. If the owners of the upper storey and the lower storey contest each other's right to the ceiling between them, or the owners of the land and the river contest each other's right to the wall between them, or two parties contest each other's right to a shirt, of which one of is holding the sleeve while the rest of it is with the other, the disputed item belongs to them both.

If a Muslim and an unbeliever contest each other's right to a corpse, each of them claiming that the deceased died as a member of his religion, then, if the true nature of his religion is known, it is attributed to him, but if it is not known, the inheritance belongs to the Muslim. If they both have proofs, the same verdict applies, but if only one of them has proof, the verdict will be in his favor on the strength thereof.

If two partners share the ownership of a slave, and one of them claims that his partner has emancipated his share, then, if they are both affluent, the slave is wholly emancipated and neither of them has any patronage *[walāʾ]* over him. If one of them is affluent and the other is impoverished, only the share of the affluent partner is emancipated. If they are both impoverished, no part of him is emancipated. If one of them purchases his partner's share, it is thereupon emancipated; it is not added to the rest, and there is no patronage over it. If each of two affluent partners claims that he has emancipated his share in a slave, they must swear to each other, and his patronage is shared by them both.

If a man says to his slave: "If I recover from this sickness of mine, you are free," or: "If I am killed, you are free," and the slave claims that he has recovered or been killed, but the heirs deny it, the word is their word. If each one of them provides proof of his statement, however, the slave is emancipated, because his proof carries more weight. If a man dies leaving two sons and two slaves of equal value, and he has no property apart from them, then, if the two sons confirm that he emancipated one of the two slaves during his death sickness, two thirds of him are emancipated, if they do not permit his total emancipation. If one of the sons says: "My father emancipated this one," but the other says: "No, he emancipated this one," one third of each of them is emancipated, and each son is entitled to a sixth of the one whose emancipation he has acknowledged, and half of the other. If the second says: "My father emancipated one of the two, but I do not know which, lots are cast between them, and lot-casting takes the place of his identification.

Chapter

Status of the Judge's Written Verdict *[Ḥukm Kitāb al-Qāḍī]*

Judgment against the absent party is permissible, provided the claimant has proof. When the judge rules against an absentee, then sends his ruling in writing to the judge of the absentee's district, it must be accepted and applied to the person against whom the verdict was given. It is not confirmed, however, except by two witnesses who say: "He read it to us," or: "It was read to him in our presence, and he said: 'Bear witness to the fact that this is my written communication to so-and-so, or to whomever it reaches among the judges of the Muslims and their governors.'" If the judge to whom it was written has died, or been dismissed from office, and it reaches someone else, the recipient must act upon it. If the writer dies or is dismissed from office after his ruling, acceptance of his written verdict is permissible. The judge's written verdict must be accepted in every case, except in cases involving legal penalties *[ḥudūd]* and retaliation *[qiṣāṣ]*.

Chapter

Partition
[Qisma]

There are two kinds of partition:

1. Partition by compulsion. This applies to property that can be divided without damage and without payment of compensation. If one of the two partners demands his portion, but the other refuses, the judge will compel him to hand it over. If they both provide him with proof of their joint ownership, and the claimant acknowledges it, he will not compel the one who refuses. If they both demand partition in this case, the property will be divided between them, and the judge will assert that its division is based on an acknowledgment, not on a proof.
2. Partition by mutual agreement. This is the partition that involves damage, in that one of the two partners cannot make use of his divided share in the property, or it cannot be repaired except with compensation from one of them, so there is no compulsion in such cases.

Partition is the distribution of a right in which there is no entitlement to preemption *[shuf'a]*, and in which no freedom of choice is established. It is permissible by weight in the case of what is measured, by measure in the case of what is weighed, and by conjectural computation in the case of fruits. The partition of a pious endowment *[waqf]* is permissible, provided that it does not involve the payment of compensation. If some of the property is unrestricted and some of it is a pious endowment, and if partition involves compensation from the owner of the unrestricted portion, it is not permissible. It is permissible, however, if it involves compensation from the owner of the pious endowment. If the parts are equal, lots are drawn over them. If someone's lot is drawn for something, it becomes his possession and that is binding.

It is imperative for the judge's partitioner to be a person of honest reputation, and likewise his notary.

The Book of Testimonies
[Kitāb ash-Shahādāt]

The Book of Testimonies
[Kitāb ash-Shahādāt]

Testimony *[shahāda]* and its performance is a collective duty *[farḍ kifāya]*.[27] If only two persons are available to undertake it, they are obliged to perform it against relatives and strangers alike, provided that is possible for them without harm, because of the saying of Allāh (Exalted is He):

O you who truly believe,	*yā ayyuha 'lladhīna āmanū*
be staunch upholders of justice,	*kūnū qawwāmīna bi'l-qisṭi*
witnesses for Allāh, even	*shuhadā'a li'llāhi wa*
though it be against yourselves	*law 'alā anfusi-kum*
or parents or kindred, whether	*awi 'l-wālidaini wa 'l-aqrabīn:*
a rich man or a poor man,	*in yakun ghaniyyan aw faqīran*
for Allāh is nearer to both. (4:135)	*fa-'llāhu awlā bi-himā.*

Matters established by testimony are of four kinds:

1. Sexual misconduct *[zinā]* and any other offense that incurs a legal penalty *[ḥadd]*, for it is not established except by [the testimony of] four men, free and equitable.
2. Property and the purposes for which property is used. This is established by [the testimony of] two male witnesses, or one man and two women, and also by one man together with the solemn oath of the claimant.
3. Apart from these two, matters that are observed by men in the majority of situations, other than acts incurring legal penalties and retaliation *[qiṣāṣ]*, such as marriage, divorce by repudiation *[ṭalāq]*, marital reunion *[raj'a]*, emancipation of slaves, appointment to office, dismissal from office, relationship, custodianship, deputyship that does not include the management of property and testamentary disposition, and similar concerns. In such cases, only two men are acceptable as witnesses.

[27] See note 25 on p. 313 above.

4. Matters that are not observed by men, such as birth, menstruation, virginity, and defects concealed beneath the clothes. These are established by the testimony of a woman of honest reputation, because ʿUqba ibn al-Ḥārith said: "Umm Yaḥyā bint Abī Ahlab got married, but a negro slave woman came to her and said: 'I suckled you both [you and your husband].' She mentioned that to the Prophet (Allāh bless him and give him peace), so he said: 'How [can you marry him] when she has made that claim [that you are his foster sister]?'"

The testimony of a male slave is accepted in relation to everything except offenses incurring legal penalties and retaliation. The testimony of a female slave is accepted in every case where the testimony of women is accepted. The following are also accepted:

- The testimony of the doer to his [or her] own deed, like that of the foster mother to her fosterage, and of the partitioner to his act of partition.
- The testimony of the brother in favor of his brother, and of the friend on behalf of his friend.
- The testimony of the deaf concerning visible things.
- The testimony of the blind man, provided that he is sound of hearing.
- The testimony of the hidden observer, and of someone who hears a person acknowledge a right, even if he does not say to the witness: "Testify about me!"
- It is permissible to testify to reports that are obviously true, and the knowledge of which is firmly established in the heart of the witness, such as testimony concerning family relationship and childbirth. That is not permissible, however, in a case involving a legal penalty or retaliation.
- The testimony of the slanderer, and others like him, is accepted after his repentance.

Chapter

Those whose testimony is rejected

The following are not accepted:

- The testimony of a minor.
- That of a person of unsound mind.
- That of a dumb mute.
- That of an unbeliever.
- That of an immoral profligate.
- That of someone whose condition is unknown.
- That of someone who gains a benefit for himself.
- That of someone who is protecting himself from harm.
- The testimony of a parent (or grandparent in any degree of ascent) in favor of his offspring, nor that of an offspring in favor of his parent.
- That of a master in favor of his slave, nor in favor of his *mukātab* [slave he has promised to emancipate for an agreed price].
- That of one of the two spouses in favor of his or her mate.
- The testimony of the trustee concerning that with which he is entrusted.
- That of the agent concerning matters assigned to his agency.
- That of the partner concerning property in which he is a partner.
- That of the enemy against his enemy.
- That of a person notorious for his frequent error and heedlessness.
- That of someone who has no chivalrous virtue, such as the laughingstock, the fellow who exposes his private parts to the onlookers in the public steam bath, and others of the kind.

If someone bears witness with a testimony that is partially suspect, the whole of it is rejected.

In cases involving challenge to the reliability of a witness, assertion of his credibility, interpretation and the like, nothing is heard except the testimony of two men. If the challenge and the favorable assertion are incompatible, the challenge takes precedence.

If a witness testifies to one thousand [units of currency], and another to two thousand, the judge will award one thousand to the claimant, and he may require him to swear together with his witness concerning the other thousand, if he sees fit. If one of them says that one thousand consists of an interest-free loan, and the other says that it represents the price of a sale, the testimony is not conclusive. If four witnesses testify to sexual misconduct, or two testify to some other offense, but they disagree about the place, or the time, or the nature of the act, their testimony is not conclusive.

Chapter

Secondary testimony concerning the original testimony, and the revocation thereof

Secondary testimony concerning the original testimony *[ash-shahāda ʿala 'sh-shahāda]* is permissible in cases where the written record of the judge's verdict is permissible, if the testimony of the original witness is unfeasible because of death, or absence, or sickness and the like, on condition that the witness of the original witness acts as his representative, saying: "I testify concerning my testimony that I am bearing witness that so-and-so affirmed in my presence, or called upon me to testify, that...."

The judge must consider what is known about the probity of both the original and the secondary witnesses. When he does not reach a verdict on the basis of the secondary testimony, but waits until the original witnesses are present, the verdict will depend on the hearing of their testimony. Then, if something emerges from any of them to prevent acceptance of the testimony, he will not judge on the basis thereof.

Subsection

Whenever a reliable witness alters his testimony, either by adding to it or subtracting from it, before the verdict is pronounced, it is accepted. If something emerges from him that prevents its acceptance after its presentation, his testimony is rejected, but if that happens after the verdict, it has no effect. If the witnesses revoke their testimony after the verdict, the verdict is not annulled, and its execution is not prevented, except in the case of prescribed penalties *[ḥudūd]* and retaliation *[qiṣāṣ]*. Such witnesses are obliged to pay compensation for whatever loss was incurred because of their testimony, in kind if it is replaceable in kind, and in value if it is not replaceable in kind. That compensation is distributed among them according to their number, so if one of them revokes, he must pay his share. If the offense to which they bore witness is a murder or the infliction of a wound, and they say: "We acted deliberately," they are subject to retaliation. If they say: "We were mistaken," they are liable for the blood money *[diya]* and the fine for wounding.

Chapter

The Oath concerning Claims
[al-Yamīn fi 'd-Daʿāwī]

The oath that is prescribed in the settlement of legal claims is the oath sworn "by Allāh (Exalted is He)," whether the person who swears is a Muslim or an unbeliever. In the case of material goods and their means of acquisition, it is permissible for judgment to be rendered on the strength of a witness and an oath, because the Prophet (Allāh bless him and give him peace) rendered judgment on the strength of a witness and an oath.

All oaths consist of the positive affirmation of fact, except the oath by which the action of another person is denied, for it consists of the negation of knowledge.

If a dead man or a bankrupt has a rightful claim, according to a witness, so the oath is sworn by the bankrupt or the heirs of the deceased, the claim is established. If he does not swear, so the oath is offered to the creditors, they are not required to swear.

If the claim is on behalf of a group, an oath is incumbent on each individual. If one says: "I shall swear a single oath for them all," it will not be accepted of him, unless they agree. If one individual claims several rights against one individual, an oath is required of him where each right is concerned.

The oath is legally prescribed in relation to every right of a human being, but it is not prescribed in relation to the rights of Allāh, such as the legal penalties *[ḥudūd]* and acts of worship.

Chapter

Acknowledgment
[Iqrār]

If a right is acknowledged by a responsible adult who is a free man, rightly guided, credible, and acting voluntarily, his acknowledgment is accepted.

If someone acknowledges a debt of dirhams [silver coins], then lapses into a silence in which it is possible for him to speak, then says: "[I mean dirhams that are] counterfeit, or small, or due at a later date," they are required of him in perfect condition, of full size, and for immediate payment. If he describes them like that in direct connection with his acknowledgment, they are required of him as described. If he excepts less than half of what he acknowledged, in direct connection with his acknowledgment, his exception is valid. If the two statements are separated by a silence in which it is possible for him to speak, or by the speech of a stranger, or if he excepts more than half of the whole amount, or of that which is different in kind, the whole amount is required of him.

If someone says: "I owe him some dirhams," then adds, "as a deposit," his statement is not accepted. If someone acknowledges a debt of [an unspecified number of] dirhams, no fewer than three are required of him, unless the person whose claim is acknowledged believes him when he says he owes less than that. If someone acknowledges a debt in general terms, his explanation is accepted according to its probability.

Subsection

The acknowledgment of a person who is not a responsible adult is not accepted in any case, with the exception of matters with which minors are permitted to deal, to the extent of the permission granted.

If a stupid fool acknowledges an offense incurring a legal penalty *[ḥadd]* or retaliation, or a divorce by repudiation, his confession is accepted. If he acknowledges a financial debt, however, his acknowledgment is not accepted. The same rule applies to the acknowledgment of a slave, unless it is connected with his financial responsibility subsequent to emancipation, except when he has been given permission to engage in trade, in which case his acknowledgment is valid to the extent of the permission granted to him.

If an invalid acknowledges a debt owed to a stranger, his acknowledgment is valid. His acknowledgment is not valid, however, if it is made during death sickness in favor of an heir, except with the confirmation of the other heirs. If he acknowledges a debt to an heir, who then becomes a non-heir, his acknowledgment is not valid. If he acknowledges a debt to him while he is a non-heir, and he then becomes an heir, his acknowledgment is valid. If a debt is due from the deceased, the heirs are not obliged to discharge it, unless he has left a legacy, in which case his debt is attached to the legacy. If the heirs prefer to discharge the debt [from their own resources] and receive the legacy intact, they are entitled to do so.

If all of the heirs acknowledge a debt owed by their legator, it is established by acknowledgment. If one of them acknowledges that debt, it is established to the extent of his right. If the deceased leaves two sons and two hundred dirhams [silver coins], and one of the two acknowledges that his father owes a debt of one hundred dīnārs [gold coins], he is obliged to pay fifty dirhams. Then, if he is honest and bears witness to his obligation, the creditor is entitled to demand his oath together with his testimony, and to receive the remainder from his brother. If the deceased leaves one son and one hundred coins, so a man claims that his father owes him one hundred, and he believes him, then another makes the same claim, and the son believes him too, if both claimants are present in a single session, the hundred is divided between them. If they are present in two sessions, however, the whole amount is awarded to the first, and nothing to the second, even if the first claimed it and the son believed him, then the other claimed it and the son believed him too, for all of it is awarded to the first and nothing to the second, who loses it because he came too late to benefit by the son's acknowledgment.

This concludes the text of *al-ʿUmda* [the Mainstay] concerning the jurisprudence of Imām Aḥmad [ibn Ḥanbal], by Imām Muwaffaq ad-Dīn ibn Qudāma.

Praise be to Allāh and to Him Alone!

About the Translator

Muhtar Holland was born in 1935, in the ancient city of Durham in the North East of England. This statement may be considered anachronistic, however, since he did not bear the name Muhtar until 1969, when he was moved—by powerful experiences in the latihan kejiwaan of Subud—to embrace the religion of Islām.*

At the age of four, according to an entry in his father's diary, he said to a man who asked his name: "I'm a stranger to myself." During his years at school, he was drawn most strongly to the study of languages, which seemed to offer signposts to guide the stranger on his "Journey Home," apart from their practical usefulness to one who loved to spend his vacations traveling—at first on a bicycle—through foreign lands. Serious courses in Latin, Greek, French, Spanish and Danish, with additional smatterings of Anglo-Saxon, Italian, German and Dutch. Travels in France, Germany, Belgium, Holland and Denmark. Then a State Scholarship and up to Balliol College, Oxford, for a degree course centered on the study of Arabic and Turkish. Travels in Turkey and Syria. Then National Service in the Royal Navy, with most of the two years spent on an intensive course in the Russian language.

In the years since graduation from Oxford and Her Majesty's Senior Service, Mr. Holland has held academic posts at the University of Toronto, Canada; at the School of Oriental and African Studies in the University of London, England (with a five-month leave to study Islamic Law in Cairo, Egypt); and at the Universiti Kebangsaan in Kuala Lumpur, Malaysia (followed by a six-month sojourn in Indonesia). He also worked as Senior Research Fellow at the Islamic Foundation in Leicester, England, and as Director of the Nūr al-Islām Translation Center in Valley Cottage, New York.

*The name Muhtar was received at that time from Bapak Muhammad Subuh Sumohadiwidjojo, of Wisma Subud, Jakarta, in response to a request for a suitable Muslim name. In strict academic transliteration from the Arabic, the spelling would be Mukhtār. The form Muchtar is probably more common in Indonesia than Muhtar, which happens to coincide with the modern Turkish spelling of the name.